Holy Walks

Holy Walks

Learning and Praying the Psalms

Stephen C. Simon

FOREWORD BY
Lynne M. Baab

WIPF & STOCK · Eugene, Oregon

HOLY WALKS
Learning and Praying the Psalms

Copyright © 2019 Stephen C. Simon. All rights reserved. Except for brief quotations in critical publications or reviews, no part of this book may be reproduced in any manner without prior written permission from the publisher. Write: Permissions, Wipf and Stock Publishers, 199 W. 8th Ave., Suite 3, Eugene, OR 97401.

Wipf & Stock
An Imprint of Wipf and Stock Publishers
199 W. 8th Ave., Suite 3
Eugene, OR 97401

www.wipfandstock.com

PAPERBACK ISBN: 978-1-5326-8800-3
HARDCOVER ISBN: 978-1-5326-8801-0
EBOOK ISBN: 978-1-5326-8802-7

Scripture quotations, unless otherwise noted, are from the New International Version of the Bible, copyright 1973, 1978, 1984, 2011 by Biblica, Inc.

Manufactured in the U.S.A.

To Carol

Thank you for being my partner all these years in this holy walk called life. Your faithfulness in following Jesus—together with your love, wisdom, discipline, and compassion—have inspired and encouraged me more than you know. I can't imagine what the journey would have been like without you.

Contents

Foreword by Lynne M. Baab | ix
Acknowledgments | xi
Introduction: Let's Go for a Walk | xiii

Chapter 1: Journeying into God's Prayer Book | 1
    An Alternative to "Shopping-List" Prayers   1
    Why Do We Pray?   7

Chapter 2: The Psalms and Walking the Dog | 12
    The Spiritual Practice of Prayer-Walking   12
    Prayer-Walking and the Psalms of Ascent   18

Chapter 3: Teaching an Old Dog a New Trick | 24
    An "Old" Pastor's New "Trick"   24
    Memorizing or Heart-Learning?   26
    How To Heart-Learn a Psalm   29

Chapter 4: A Walking Conversation | 37
    Addressing God in the Psalms   39
        Names for God in the Psalms   42
        Are All the Psalms Prayers?   44
    Hearing God Through the Psalms   46
        Understanding the Nature of God's Voice   48
        Learning To Recognize God's Voice   51

CONTENTS

Chapter 5: Exercising the Heart | 54
    Getting Acquainted with the Psalms 55
    Introduction to Hebrew Poetry 62
        Comparing English and Hebrew Poetry 64
        Some Definitions in Hebrew Poetry 66
        Parallelism 67
        Imagery and Metaphor 70
        Acrostic Psalms 74

Chapter 6: Rain or Shine, You Gotta Go Out! | 76
    The Psalms as Prayers for Every Day 76
    Psalms of Trust 81
    Wisdom Psalms 85
    Sacred Story Psalms 90

Chapter 7: What If It's Dark and Storming? | 97
    Psalms of Lament 97
    Praying with Brutal Honesty 104
    Praying into Grace 106

Chapter 8: The Journey's Destination | 111
    Psalms of Praise 111
        A Masterpiece of Praise to God 114
    Praising God: What Are We Really Doing? 116
    Praising God for Ever and Ever 120

Chapter 9: A Panoramic View | 127
    God as Our Creator 129
    God as Our Leader 135
    God as Our Rescuer 143

Next Steps | 151

Appendix: The Psalms I'm Heart-Learning . . . | 157
Bibliography | 163

Foreword

WHEN I READ A psalm—or listen to a sung version of a psalm—I am invited into something amazing and wonderful. The Psalms encourage me to approach God just as I am, with my messy emotions and disordered thoughts. The psalm writers model an extreme honesty before God that lightens my heart. I see that I, too, can be honest, that God welcomes my anger, frustration, sadness, and pain. Whatever has caused these emotions, however much I blame myself for feeling these things, God says, "Come."

When I stay in a psalm, something else happens, equally wonderful and freeing. In almost every psalm, God turns negative emotions into praise, thankfulness, joy and singing. "Weeping may linger for the night, but joy comes with the morning" (Psalm 30:5, NRSV). For me, the period of weeping is often much shorter than a night because the psalm writers' words lighten my heart as I pray along with them.

Steve Simon knows this. In *Holy Walks*, Steve describes the ways he has grown in becoming a person who loves God with his heart, not just his mind. Steve is one of the smartest people I know, and it has been a delight to the see the ways the Psalms have taken Steve's faith from his mind into his whole being.

Steve's fine mind is visible in *Holy Walks*, as he explains the variety of types of psalms, how psalms are structured, and how the language of the psalms works. But even more valuable is Steve's description of the specific habits that enable him to engage with the psalms: memorizing specific psalms, pondering them, and praying them—while he walks his dog.

Memorizing passages in the Bible has been a key practice for me. The passages I know by heart have shaped me deeply. They have given me fodder for thought and prayer. They have helped me draw near to God. Countless other Christians throughout the ages have benefitted from memorizing portions of the Bible, and each person who wants to memorize scriptural passages has to come up with a system for doing it.

Steve provides helpful specifics for how he memorizes psalms. His method may well be beneficial for many readers.

The walking component of Steve's engagement with the Psalms is also significant. Christians have long underemphasized the significance of the body, and I am thrilled that in recent years Christians have begun to rediscover spiritual practices based in the body, including fasting, pilgrimage, walking a labyrinth, and the stations of the cross. Friends increasingly tell me they are finding joy in a variety of bodily positions while praying. The rhythm of my feet hitting the pavement has always enabled prayer to flow easily for me, and I love Steve's combination of walking while memorizing, pondering and praying the Psalms.

The strong presence of Emma, Steve's beloved dog, adds lightness and humor to *Holy Walks*. The dog, the varied weather, the early morning air—Steve has grounded his book beautifully in the physical world made by God, the Creation mentioned so frequently and so tenderly in the Psalms.

Steve calls the Psalms a "remedy for lifeless prayer." Amen to that! As I pray along with the psalm writers, I get to experience such a range of prayer forms and moods. In times of trouble, the Psalms help me experience God restoring my peace and joy. And as I pray outside in nature, I experience something wonderful about God's creativity in our beautiful world.

Because the Psalms, scripture memory, and praying while walking have been such important aspects of my faith journey, I can enthusiastically tell you that if you adopt some or all of Steve's method as he describes it in *Holy Walks*, you will grow in intimacy with God.

—Rev. Lynne M. Baab, PhD, author of *Sabbath Keeping* and
Joy Together: Spiritual Practices for Your Congregation

Acknowledgments

THIS BOOK WOULD NOT exist if I had not been given the privilege of teaching, preaching, and discussing the ideas and material in *Holy Walks* with numerous groups of people during the past eight years. The teacher always learns more than the students, and the people who've sat under my teaching have taught me much, sharpened my thinking, and motivated me to continue exploring the Psalms. I'm especially grateful to the wonderful folks at Forest Grove Reformed Church in Hudsonville, Michigan, where this adventure with the Psalms began; at Community Reformed Church in Zeeland, Michigan, where the book's outline took shape in the adult classes I taught; and at Shadle Park Presbyterian Church, where my wife and I settled after we moved to Spokane and where I've been able to teach about the Psalms from the pulpit, in the classroom, and in several small groups. Since coming to eastern Washington, I've also taught portions of this material to other congregations in the area through sermons and classes, as well as through guest lectures at Whitworth University. I'm thankful for all of these more recent opportunities as well. They've enabled me to refine—and hopefully improve—the material in this book.

Going back further, this book also would never have come about if not for the many, many faithful disciples of Jesus who've mentored me through all my years of walking with our Lord, as well as those who've ministered with me (and, frequently, to me) in the service of our Lord. I can't possibly name them all, but please know that I am grateful for each of you who has been a part of that great cloud of witnesses for me.

I'm also deeply grateful to my wife Carol and my friends, Lynne Baab, Ben Brody, and Dann Stouten, who generously read early versions of the manuscript and provided feedback, ideas, and editing. Your encouragement was invaluable, and your numerous suggestions were always much appreciated even when I chose not to follow some of them. A very special

ACKNOWLEDGMENTS

thanks as well to Lynne for contributing the gracious foreword to this book. Lynne, I have long found your writings and thoughts on spiritual disciplines, prayer, and the Psalms to be extremely insightful and uplifting. I hope you recognize your influence throughout this book.

I also want to thank the wise editors at Wipf and Stock Publishers, for their work in turning my manuscript into an actual paper-and-ink book. Without them, *Holy Walks* would exist only in the memory banks of my computer and perhaps a few places in the cloud. So, thank you, Jim, Matt, Daniel, and the rest of your talented gang.

Finally, I want to acknowledge my canine walking partner, Emma, whom you'll meet in numerous stories throughout the book. After thousands of miles of walking with me, Emma crossed over the Rainbow Bridge shortly after the original manuscript was completed. Although I have a new canine walking partner now, Emma will never be forgotten. Truly an angel on four paws, her faithful companionship honored her Creator. We should all be so blessed.

Introduction

Let's Go for a Walk

> "Blessed is the one
> who does not walk in step with the wicked
> or stand in the way that sinners take
> or sit in the company of mockers,
> but whose delight is in the law of the Lord,
> and who meditates on his law day and night."
>
> —Psalm 1:1–2[1]

Seven a.m.

The sky brightens, and another day dawns. I've eaten breakfast, and now I'm preparing for the next part of my morning routine: walking the dog.

As I click the leash on her collar, Emma's stubby tail wags her entire body. Emma is my orange-and-white Brittany Spaniel. She's well up in years now, but she's still eager for another adventure out on the streets and sidewalks near our home. She pulls me out the door, on our way to get a little exercise and so she can do her business.

It's also my time for praying the Psalms.

As we walk along, Emma explores her world of smells and sniffs with an enthusiasm and single-minded focus I can only admire. Meanwhile, I quietly recite psalms that I've learned during our previous walks. The words and thoughts of the various psalms become my words and thoughts. In a mysterious way I'll never understand, they flow from the recesses of my

---

1. All Scripture references in this book are taken from the *New International Version* (2011) unless otherwise indicated.

mind into my heart, then out to my mouth, and, ultimately, I believe, to the ears of God himself. Walking along in a conversation with the One who created me, I listen for the thoughts and ideas the Spirit puts in my mind as I prayerfully recite one psalm and then another. To an observer, it may look simply like a man walking his dog. But we're not alone. God's presence transforms my steps into a *holy walk*.

On most days, Emma and I go on one or two of these holy walks. They vary in length from fifteen to forty-five minutes, and we generally cover one to two miles. We certainly don't set any speed records. Afterwards, naptime beckons Emma, but I know that for those few minutes I've had the privilege of being with God in a special way. On occasion, I sense that God has spoken to me about something particular. Most of the time, I simply feel renewed energy to move into whatever the next few hours hold for me. Always, I know that God has been at work in my heart and, for a short while at least, I've been drawn a bit closer to God. In my lighter moments, I also wonder if, perhaps, Emma has even become a slightly more righteous dog. After all, I suspect she's heard more prayers than the average dog. Plus, she does occasionally attempt to put the fear of God into unsuspecting squirrels. (Maybe she's a wannabe evangelist?)

I've been walking with Jesus for nearly fifty years—since my high school days—and Emma and I have walked together for most of her short life. But I'm almost ashamed to say that I only began praying the Psalms about eight years ago. Oh, I've always had my favorite psalms, of course—just as I'm sure you have. I've also turned to various psalms when I've gone through hard times. As a pastor, I've even preached on my share of psalms. But praying the Psalms? For me, that's only been a recent discovery. But what a marvelous discovery it's been! And it's one I would like the privilege of sharing with you.

In this book, I'm inviting you to walk alongside me in my own personal journey with the Psalms. You'll get an inside look at what I've been learning about praying the Psalms. The Psalms have become my friends and companions, my teachers and mentors, my personal trainers and accountability partners. As I've gotten to know them, they've transformed my prayer life and revitalized and deepened my walk with God—and I believe they can do that for you as well.

As we walk together through these pages, I'll lead us in examining numerous psalms and reflecting on various theological topics. I'll also provide some suggestions for your own devotional practices. Through it all, however, I have this straightforward purpose in mind: *To enable you to walk more closely with God by using the Psalms to enrich your understanding and practice of prayer.* My desire is that God will use this book to continue the good work I'm confident God's already been doing in your life. Thus, even while I've been writing, I've been praying that my words will lead you to fall in love with the Psalms, as I have. Nothing would delight me more than for you to develop a love affair with the Psalms and experience the joy and wonder of God's heart as you pray the Psalms.

With that goal in mind, here's a brief roadmap of where we'll be going on this journey into the Psalms:

First, in chapter 1, I'll share with you how I fell into this newfound love for the Psalms. It wasn't something I set out to do, but looking back on the past few years, God was obviously at work in my heart. Each of our journeys with God is unique, but we can often find encouragement for our own walk when we hear the stories of others. I hope my story will do that for you.

In chapters 2 and 3 I'll examine the two spiritual practices that I've integrated into my journey with the Psalms. The first one is prayer-walking, and the second is memorizing Scripture (or "heart-learning," as I prefer to call it; I'll explain why in chapter 3). Certainly, many people have long practiced either or both of these two disciplines—perhaps you have as well—but what I've done is combine them with praying the Psalms, which is a spiritual practice of its own, of course. This has produced the kind of hybrid spiritual practice (holy walks) that I've found to be so fruitful and rewarding—and one that I hope you'll be challenged to try for yourself.

We often think of prayer as a monologue, but in chapter 4 I'll advocate for the idea that prayer is actually a conversation with God. I'll look at what the Psalms teach us about addressing God, and I'll also share with you what I've been learning about hearing God, about listening for and recognizing God's gentle whispers. Listening is always the hardest part for me, and probably for most of us. We're often in such a hurry to tell God what's on our minds that we rarely stop and listen to what's on God's mind. However, it's the conversational aspect that makes holy walks truly holy, so we need to learn to listen to God as well.

In chapter 5 I'll present some general background information about the Psalms, including a short introduction to Hebrew poetry. You don't need to be a biblical scholar to pray the Psalms, but a certain level of knowledge and understanding about the Psalms will be useful and will help you appreciate them that much more. This chapter will provide that.

In chapters 6–8 I'll discuss five primary types of psalms. All of the psalms are poems (rather than narratives, letters, or some other literary genre), but they're poems with varied styles and themes, because they reflect the different needs and purposes of each psalmist. In these three chapters I'll look at the characteristics of five major kinds of psalms: Psalms of Trust, Wisdom Psalms, Sacred Story Psalms, Psalms of Lament, and Praise Psalms. Most importantly, I'll explain how God uses each of these types of psalms in our hearts as we learn them and pray them.

The book of Psalms is not a systematic theology, but it does reveal much about God and God's relationship with his people. In chapter 9, I'll pull some themes together and provide an overview of the Psalms and what they teach us about God as our Creator, Leader, and Rescuer.

Finally, I'll wrap up the journey (at least in this book) with a few suggestions for the "Next Steps" you might want to take in setting out on your own adventures with the Psalms. My hope is that by the time you make your way through this book you'll have already started going on some holy walks of your own. This final section will give you some suggestions for how you can keep growing in this spiritual practice.

So that's the journey I'll be leading you on. Before we set off, I should emphasize that this is a book for people who are (or who want to be) disciples of Jesus Christ. But don't let that scare you off. After all, a disciple is a learner, not an expert, so I'm not assuming you have lots of biblical knowledge. Nor do I assume you already have a strong and vibrant relationship with God. What I am assuming is that you desire to follow our Lord Jesus and that you want to love him with all your heart, soul, mind, and strength. That's the essence of being a disciple. Disciples are always seeking to become more faithful followers and lovers of God. So if you're reading this book, I'm assuming you're serious about wanting to know God better and to grow in your walk with God.

For that reason, I want this book to impact your heart as well as your head. So, as we go along, I'll be encouraging you to do some personal reflection and exploring of the Psalms on your own. Questions and exercises to help you do that are found in sections labeled "Extra Steps." Please don't skip over these. Instead, extend your "walk" through this book a little bit and make time for these "extra steps." You'll get much more out of the journey if you'll do that.

To get the most out of this book, you'll also need to have a Bible with you as you read. I'll be discussing numerous psalms, as well as referring to other biblical texts, and most of the time I've chosen not to print the text of the psalm under discussion. So it's important for you to have a Bible close at hand. For those of us who wish to be apprentices of the Master Carpenter, the Bible is an essential tool—just as a hammer or saw is for regular carpenters—and we need to learn to use it well. So keep your Bible handy while you read—and be sure to take the time to look up the psalms and references that are discussed or cited.

Another way to get more out of this book is to read it along with a friend, or with your spouse, if you're married. That way you can encourage each other through mutual accountability and by learning from each other's experiences and insights with the Psalms. Or perhaps your small group would be interested in using this book to explore the Psalms together, reading and discussing a chapter a week. Or you might consider using this book to mentor another Jesus-follower. Just set a regular time and place to meet and discuss the various chapters and topics together—perhaps at your favorite coffee shop, student union, or local restaurant. You'll have to provide the beverage of choice, but the "Extra Steps" sections can help you interact together with the material along the way.

Before we get started on this journey into learning and praying the Psalms, I want to say a word about the imagery of dogs and dog walking, which runs throughout the book. You'll discover that my dog Emma makes frequent appearances, and you may wonder why I've chosen to combine a discussion of prayer and the Bible with something as earthy and mundane as walking a dog. The simple answer is that this was how I learned to pray the Psalms. From the very beginning, I've learned to pray the Psalms while walking my dog, and the two activities have gone together for me in a delightful and fun way. Another reason to write about these two activities together is that dogs can teach us much about faithfulness, joy, unconditional love, and other spiritual qualities. While such canine lessons aren't the focus of this book, some of those will undoubtedly show through anyway.

However, what sealed my decision to employ the dog-walking imagery in this discussion is that I believe it fits well with the teaching style of Jesus himself. Admittedly, Jesus didn't talk much about dogs in his teaching, although they did figure prominently in one fascinating back-and-forth repartee that he had with a Gentile woman (Mark 7:24–30). I suspect this is because dogs didn't become household pets until the early part of the twentieth century, and in Jesus' day, they were generally viewed in a negative way. The word "dog" was even used as a common slur to demean Gentiles, which may be another reason he avoided talking about dogs.

But even if Jesus didn't often refer to dogs, I wonder if you've noticed how regularly he incorporated other animals into his teaching? For instance, sheep were perhaps even more omnipresent in his day than dogs are in ours, and several times Jesus referred to them in his teaching.[2] Jesus also added life to his teaching by talking about birds (Matt. 5:26, 10:16, and Luke 12:6 and 24), a hen with her chicks (Matt. 23:37), wolves (Matt. 7:15), and camels (Matt. 19:24). In the latter instance, Jesus was even cracking a joke, using a camel as the central figure.

So Jesus often turned to the animal kingdom for illustration material. He also spoke regularly about ordinary chores and tasks, such as sowing seeds (Mark 4:3–8), fishing (Mark 1:17), and sweeping a house (Luke 15:8–10). Since his audience readily understood everyday activities like these, Jesus used them to explain deeper truths about life and discipleship. Today, many of us are well-acquainted with the everyday job of walking a dog. So in using dog walks to teach about praying the Psalms, I'm simply seeking to follow Jesus' example. I believe he would wholeheartedly approve.

With those thoughts in mind, we're ready to begin our adventures with the Psalms. As we set out together, allow me to offer this prayer for you:

> *Loving and Merciful God, I thank you for the person who's reading these words right now. No matter where they are in their relationship with you, or however long they've walked with you, I pray that you will bless them as they make their way through this book. May you speak to them and reveal yourself more fully to them through the Psalms, and may they fall in love with the book of Psalms, even as I have. Through the Psalms, speak your Word, not just to their mind, but especially to their heart. Help them delight in your Word and find joy in the practice of learning and praying the Psalms. Lead them on a holy walk through life. But even more than all that, Gracious Lord, I pray that through the Psalms, they might grow closer to you, the One who created each of us, who leads us through all of life, and who rescues us again and again. Amen.*

---

2. E.g., Matt. 10:16, 18:12–15, Luke 10:3, 15:4–7, and, especially, John 10:1–16, where Jesus likens himself to a shepherd caring for his sheep.

Extra Steps:

Why did you pick up this book? Why did it intrigue you or interest you?

Now that you've read this brief introduction and outline of where we're headed, what do you think will be most helpful to you? What are you most eager to learn?

Take a moment to reflect on the current state of your relationship with God. Then ask God to use this book in specific ways in your walk with him.

Chapter 1

Journeying into God's Prayer Book

*"Come and hear, all you who fear God,
and I will tell what he has done for my soul."*

—Psalm 66:16 (English Standard Version)

An Alternative to "Shopping-List" Prayers

Has a sermon ever had a life-changing impact on you? Have you ever heard a sermon that caused you to make some major change in your life, in your thinking, or in your relationship with God?

I can point to a sermon in the fall of 2011 that had a huge impact on my life and my walk with God. In fact, I remember it quite well—because I preached it. I don't know what kind of impact that sermon may have had on anyone else, but it kicked off a season of tremendous spiritual growth for me. I didn't realize it at the time, but that sermon was the beginning of my adventures with the Psalms. Since then, I've studied, prayed, and memorized ("heart-learned") many, many psalms. Along the way, I've come to view prayer in new ways. And, most importantly, I've been growing in my love for God.

But I'm getting ahead of the story. Let me tell you how that sermon came about.

I was the Minister of Discipleship at a medium-sized church in the farm country of Hudsonville, Michigan, and we had decided to have a year-long, congregational emphasis on prayer. During the year, we would have classes on prayer, a prayer workshop, newsletter articles about prayer, and small groups studying various prayers in the Bible. In my staff role, I only preached about once a month, but I was scheduled for one of the

Sundays early in that "prayer year." So, naturally, I wanted my sermon to be about prayer.

But what should I say about prayer? You've undoubtedly heard a lot of sermons on prayer, and so have I. I didn't want to simply tell the people that prayer is important or that we should pray more. We all know *that*. So I wrestled with what I should say in that sermon. . . .

Extra Steps:

If you had the opportunity to talk to a group of people about prayer, what would you want to tell them? What do you think is the most important aspect of prayer? What have you personally learned about prayer that you would want to share with others?

Like many people, my wife Carol and I keep a shopping list on our refrigerator. Whenever we run out of something, we add it to the list. Then, when there are enough crucial items on the list, we take it down and one of us heads for the grocery store. As I looked ahead to that upcoming sermon, I reflected on my own prayer life, and I realized that my prayers often resembled those long shopping lists. And they were just about as exciting. Item after item after item after item: "God, please bless Carol. Be with Matt and Julie, and with Paul and Julie. Please strengthen Jim. Bless our Bible study group. Watch over my friends. . . ." Etc. Etc. My prayers felt like long shopping lists that I brought before the Lord.

I rarely felt inspired by those prayers. Nor did they bring me closer to God. Too often they lacked a sense of life and the Spirit. Plus, God knew all about the items on my list anyway, so what was I really accomplishing by listing them for him yet one more time? Shopping-list prayers just didn't cut it for me. And I suspected I wasn't the only person who struggled with that. Perhaps you do as well.

I concluded that I needed an alternative to shopping-list prayers. So that's what I decided to preach about. After all, the best sermons are those that we preachers preach to ourselves before we ever preach them to our congregations. That was certainly true for this sermon.

I chose Psalm 145 as the biblical text for the sermon, and on that Sunday morning I shared with the congregation how God was teaching me to focus less on a long list of prayer concerns and to spend more time praising God and seeking God's heart. I explained how praising God can transform our shopping-list prayers. After I finished giving the sermon, I invited the congregation to read Psalm 145 together with me as our closing prayer.

That sermon was the first step of my journey into the Psalms. At the time, I thought praising God was the antidote to shopping-list prayers. But what I've come to learn since then is that *praying the Psalms* is a remedy for lifeless prayers. Praising God is part of the answer, but there's so much more as well.

Before I began this journey into the Psalms, I would probably have described the book of Psalms as a rather haphazard collection of Hebrew poems and prayers: some very moving and inspirational, some rather odd and strange, and a few that seem almost un-Christian. And all of that is certainly true. But since then, I've discovered something that many, many people have already known. (I'm often a little late to the party.) Perhaps you've known it as well. What I've discovered is that *the book of Psalms is nothing less than God's Prayer Book.*

What I've learned is that God didn't lead the biblical writers to include the Psalms in the Bible just to inspire us. Nor are the Psalms intended just to encourage us during our down times. That's important, sure, but the Psalms have a much larger purpose than just providing a little spiritual pick-me-up. No, God provided the book of Psalms to teach his people—to teach *us*—how to pray. That's why the book of Psalms is rightly called "God's Prayer Book." It isn't just a *collection* of prayers. It's a *guidebook* for learning how to pray.

Now, God's Prayer Book doesn't teach us how to pray in the way an instruction manual might teach us how to tune our lawnmower or knit a cardigan. It doesn't give us *Five Easy Steps to a Better Prayer Life*. Nor does it answer a lot of our theological questions about prayer. Instead, God's Prayer Book teaches us how to pray in much the way that a parent teaches a child how to speak.

Ben Patterson explains this analogy very well in his book on the Psalms.[1] Patterson notes that babies are quite capable of expressing their desires with all kinds of grunts and squeals and cries. That isn't the same as speaking, of course. But soon babies begin to mimic what they hear from their parents. Then, over time, that mimicking develops meaning, and the children begin weaving words and ideas together with syntax and grammar. And thus children learn to speak. They learn to speak the language of their parents.

---

1. Patterson, *God's Prayer Book*, 1–2.

That's what the book of Psalms does for us. The Psalms teach us to speak to God in God's own language, which is the language of prayer. In his delightful little book, *Psalms: The Prayer Book of the Bible*, Dietrich Bonhoeffer also notes that parents teach their children to speak by speaking to and with them. Then he points out, "So we learn to speak to God because God has spoken to us and speaks to us. By means of the speech of the Father in heaven his children learn to speak with him. Repeating God's own words after him, we begin to pray to him."[2]

What Bonhoeffer and Patterson (and others) are saying is that prayer is not something that you and I just instinctively know how to do. Rather, prayer is always a response to God's speech. If God never spoke to us, we would never know how to pray to God. In fact, we would never even guess that we ought to pray, or that we could pray. Prayer is answering speech, as Eugene Peterson explains: "The Psalms are acts of obedience, answering the God who has addressed us. God's word precedes these words; these prayers don't seek God, they respond to the God who seeks us."[3]

Peterson's words echo those of O. Hallesby in his spiritual classic, *Prayer*, written decades earlier. Attempting to describe what prayer is, Hallesby quotes Revelation 3:20, "Here I am! I stand at the door and knock. If anyone hears my voice and opens the door, I will come in and eat with that person, and they with me." Then he states,

> I doubt that I know of a passage in the whole Bible which throws greater light upon prayer than this one does. It is, it seems to me, the key which opens the door into the holy and blessed realm of prayer.... It is Jesus who moves us to pray. He knocks. Thereby He makes known His desire to come in to us. Our prayers are always a result of Jesus' knocking at our hearts' doors.[4]

In his book, *Learning To Pray Through the Psalms*, Jim Sire tells how he first came to understand this "answering speech" nature of the Psalms.[5] On one occasion, he had opened his Bible at random to Psalm 108, where he read, "My heart is ready, O God. My heart is ready." He immediately sensed that those words were describing the state of his own heart and that they were the precise words he wanted to speak to God. In other words, by

---

2. Bonhoeffer, *Psalms*, 11.
3. Peterson, *Answering God*, 5.
4. Hallesby, *Prayer*, 11.
5. Sire, *Learning To Pray*, 11.

praying that particular psalm, Sire found himself using its words to answer God, who had first spoken those words to him.

So as we spend time listening to God speak to us in the Psalms, we learn how to answer God, how to speak back to him. We learn to pray by listening to God and learning God's language. To reiterate Bonhoeffer's insight: "Repeating God's own words after him, we begin to pray to him."[6] And that's why the book of Psalms is God's Prayer Book.

But learning a language does more than just enable us to speak. As Patterson also points out, language actually changes who we are and makes us more than just a babbling baby or a demanding child.[7] Think back again to the analogy of a child learning to talk. Certainly, language enables the child to express his or her desires. But, much more importantly, by learning the language of the parents, the child also learns the parents' desires and values and culture and is, in turn, shaped by them.

Reflect on that for a moment. Isn't that true for anyone who learns another language? When we learn to speak another language, we begin to understand the people who speak that language. Not just their words, but we begin to understand their culture, their way of thinking, their heart, and their mind.

For instance, when I was in seminary, I had to learn Hebrew (the original language of the Old Testament) and Greek (the original language of the New Testament). I never became more than a novice in either of those biblical languages, but I learned enough to see how the languages themselves would have shaped the people who spoke them. For instance, Hebrew is built on the verbs, and it's a very picturesque language. I could see how it was a natural for the poetry of the Psalms and the Prophets. On the other hand, Greek is much more complex and precise, and I could easily understand why it was the language of ancient philosophers and theologians. The Apostle Paul's letter to the Romans is an amazing work of theology, but I suspect it would have been difficult for him to write it in Hebrew. However, the Greek language allows the kind of nuanced arguments and reasoning that characterize Romans (as well as Paul's other writings). By learning those two biblical languages, I learned something about the people of the Bible as well.

---

6. Bonhoeffer, *Psalms*, 11.

7. Patterson, *God's Prayer Book*, 2.

Extra Steps:

If you're able to speak another language, how does that help you better understand the people who are native speakers of that language? What insights does their language give you into their life and culture and their way of thinking? Can you think of ways that those insights have shaped your own thinking or behavior?

In the same way, when we learn God's language, the language of prayer, we learn about God. We learn God's desires for us. We learn God's values and priorities. We learn God's heart. And we pray in response. Learning God's language changes us so that we become men and women after God's own heart.

This is the way God's people have learned to pray for thousands of years. As Peterson points out, "When we pray the Psalms, and are trained in prayer by them, we enter the centuries-long experience of being God's people."[8] In other words, when we pray the Psalms, we're praying some of the same prayers that God's people have prayed since at least the time of King David (approximately 1000 BC).

The book of Psalms is also how the disciples learned to pray: Peter, James, John, and all the rest. In fact, have you ever considered that this is also how Jesus himself learned to pray? Jesus had to learn to pray, to talk with his heavenly Father, just like you and I do. And he did that through the book of Psalms, through God's Prayer Book. I can easily picture Mary and Joseph tucking the young boy Jesus into bed at night and quietly coaxing him to sleep by reciting their favorite psalms. I also can see Jesus as a teenager, sitting in the synagogue listening to rabbis read the Psalms and use the Psalms to lead the people in prayer.

The biblical scholar N. T. Wright points out that Jesus, Paul, and all the other early disciples would have grown up with the Psalms as their "hymnbook" and would have known them "inside out" and "by heart." As a result, Wright summarizes, "What Jesus believed and understood about his own identity and vocation, and what Paul came to believe and understand about Jesus' unique achievement, they believed and understood within a psalm-shaped world."[9]

---

8. Peterson, *Answering God*, 17.
9. Wright, *Case for the Psalms*, 11.

And so that's what I've come to understand and love about the book of Psalms—in a way that I don't think I ever really did before. Since giving that sermon on Psalm 145, I've spent a great deal of time with the Psalms. I've studied them, I've preached on them, I've heard other pastors preach on them, and I've also memorized many of them. Those psalms have become my daily prayers, and I've prayed many of them hundreds of times during the past several years. As I've done that, I've been learning the language of prayer in a deeper way than I've ever known before. As those psalms have sunk into my mind and then into my heart and soul, they've drawn me closer to the heart of God.

That's a long, long way from those old shopping-list prayers.

Extra Steps:

With a friend, talk about your previous experiences with the Psalms. Here are some questions to get you started:

- Do you have a favorite psalm? If so, which one is it and why do you like it so much?
- When have you personally turned to the Psalms?
- How have you seen the Psalms used in worship services?
- Have you ever been in a class or Bible study on the Psalms? Describe it. What do you remember learning from the class?

Why Do We Pray?

Thinking about prayer reminds me of one of my favorite stories about prayer, a story that comes from, of all places, a football locker room.

Perhaps you're familiar with Mike Ditka from his work in recent years as a football commentator on Sunday afternoons. However, in the 1980s, Ditka was the head coach for the Chicago Bears, one of the most dominating football teams of all time and winners of the 1985 Super Bowl. Ken Davis recounts a story that was told to him by John Cassis, who served as a kind of chaplain to the team in those days.[10]

Coach Ditka was getting ready to give a pre-game pep talk to the team. As he surveyed his players, Ditka spotted defensive tackle William

---

10. Davis, *Lighten Up*, 136.

Perry, who had the extremely apt nickname of "The Fridge." Weighing in at well over 300 pound, Perry was huge even for a pro football player. For a brief time, Ditka experimented with using the Fridge as a running back, because . . . , well, can you imagine trying to tackle a 300-pound running back? Looking to use him in a less-obvious way, Ditka—who's a religious man—said to the Fridge, "When I finish, I'd like you to close with the Lord's Prayer." Then he began his pep talk, as Cassis and the players listened intently.

Meanwhile, the Bears' star quarterback, Jim McMahon, leaned over to Cassis and whispered, "Look at Fridge!" Cassis glanced over at Perry, who was holding his head in his hands, sweating and obviously in great agony. "He doesn't know the Lord's Prayer!" Cassis wasn't sure what was going on, but he whispered back to McMahon, "*Everybody* knows the Lord's Prayer." After a short pause, McMahon leaned over to Cassis yet again. "I'll bet you fifty bucks *Fridge* doesn't know the Lord's Prayer." (When Cassis told the story later on, he commented on how weird it felt to be betting on the Lord's Prayer!)

The Fridge may have wished that Ditka's talk would never end, but eventually it did, and Ditka nodded at him. As the coach bowed his head, silence overtook the entire room. Then the Fridge began to speak in a small, shaky voice, "Now I lay me down to sleep, I pray the Lord my soul to keep. . . ."

Just then, Cassis felt a tap on his shoulder. He turned, and McMahon handed him a fifty-dollar bill and said, "I had no idea Fridge knew the Lord's Prayer!"

I love that story. Prayer has a way of humbling all of us, doesn't it? We've all gotten prayers mixed up at times, or bumbled our words, or didn't know what to pray. I've never made the particular mistake the Fridge did, but I have messed up the Lord's Prayer on occasion. Once, I was leading a congregation in praying it, and I left out the whole part about forgiving our debts. Afterwards, I referred to that as the *Lord's Prayer Lite*. You know, fewer requests, fewer calories.

As we think together about prayer, can I ask you a question before we push on with this journey into the Psalms? It's a rather personal question, but I think it's extremely important. Unless we have an answer to this question, the Psalms will never have the impact on our lives that God intends. So, before we go on to discuss spiritual practices with the Psalms, ask yourself this question: *Why do I pray?* Before you read on, take a few moments to reflect on that question.

Extra Steps:

Reflect on your own experience with prayer. Why do you pray?

What do you think is the purpose for prayer?

Is that what actually motivates your own praying? If not, what does?

Numerous surveys indicate that the vast majority of people pray, at least on occasion. Even some atheists profess to pray at times—although one wonders to Whom or to What they think they're praying. Prayers take place before meals, by bedsides, in church sanctuaries, before meetings, in war zones, in airplanes, in dorm rooms, in special prayer closets, and countless other places. But what motivates all those prayers?

Over the years I've talked with many people about prayer, and I've done considerable reflection on my own prayer practices. Here are four common reasons why many of us pray, if we're honest with ourselves:

- For many of us, we see prayer as our *duty*, as something we're expected to do. In other words, we pray simply because we're supposed to pray. We don't really ask why we pray. We just do it. Perhaps a parent or a pastor taught us that when we were very young, and we've simply never bothered to question it. We pray because that's what God's people are supposed to do.

- For some people, prayer can best be described as a *habit*. We pray stock prayers out of habit before a meal or before bedtime. Or we recite the Rosary or the Lord's Prayer (the *full* version, not the *lite* version). While these prayers can certainly have great value, the danger of habitual prayers is that they can become mindless prayers. We can pray them without really thinking about them.

- Another reason we might pray is to *feel better*. When we're anxious, worried, or afraid, prayer can be a way to find comfort and to feel better about ourselves, about the world, or about life. While prayer often produces peace and a more confident outlook on our circumstances, what if it doesn't? We can't always measure the effectiveness of our prayers by how they make us feel.

- Perhaps the most common reason for praying is to *get things*. Prayer is how we ask God to do things for ourselves, for loved ones, for friends, and even for complete strangers. Even people who aren't especially devoted to prayer will pray when they feel desperate enough. However, focusing on our needs and desires in prayer often leads to those shopping-list prayers I talked about earlier.

Now, there's certainly some justification for each of these motivations. Christians should pray, and a Christian who never prays probably ought to question his or her relationship with God. Learning to pray habitually is necessary for developing us into women and men of prayer. God frequently blesses our prayer times by giving us a sense of peace or love or some other emotion. And Jesus himself told us to bring our requests to our heavenly Father. So we can't say it's wrong to pray out of duty, or habit, or to experience a certain feeling, or to get things.

But what does it say about our understanding of prayer if we pray *only* out of duty, or habit, or a desire for a certain feeling, or when our prayers are just spiritualized versions of a shopping list? After all, imagine what a marriage would be like if the husband and wife only spoke to each other when they felt they had a duty to do so? Or what if a husband had a habit of saying "I love you" to his wife but never put any emotion or thought into the words? Or what if each spouse only did something for their loved one if they felt better for doing it? Or what if the only time the wife spoke to her husband was to put another item on his "Honey Do" list? If we're not careful, we can treat God like that in our prayer life.

However, God designed prayer to be one of the primary ways that we deepen our relationship with him. As Bill Hybels has written, "The most intimate communion with God comes only through prayer."[11] Duty, habit, feelings, or need may explain why we actually do pray, but our ultimate motive for praying should be *to grow in our communion with God*. Through prayer we enter into a relationship with God. Through prayer we share our heart with God and we learn about God's heart, including God's values, priorities, and desires. Through prayer God gradually shapes our heart to be more and more like his. Through prayer we grow in faith and love for God. Through prayer we gain spiritual strength and learn faithful obedience. Through prayer we become more open and available to God. In such

---

11. Hybels, *Too Busy*, 8.

ways, prayer, more than just about anything else, enables us to grow deeper in our relationship with God.

So the overarching purpose for praying should be to know God better. If that isn't the desire of our heart, then we're just playing with prayer. We're like someone who's been given a Lamborghini but only uses it to drive to the grocery store. Or who has a grand piano in their living room but never learns to play anything besides *Chopsticks*. Or who has a full woodworking shop but only makes kindling for the fireplace. Sadly, too many of us do just that. I know that's been true for me at times. Perhaps for you as well.

That's where praying the Psalms has come in for me. The Psalms are God's Prayer Book, and as I've been learning to pray them, my heart has been drawn to God in ever deeper ways. When I pray the Psalms, I sense that I'm in the very presence of God himself. Elmer Towns compares the Psalms to mirrors. As we gaze into the Psalms, they reflect back to us all the sin and spiritual junk that's in our heart. But they also show us what a godly life truly looks like, and as we continue to look deeper into each mirror, we see God himself.[12] In other words, praying the Psalms—gazing into these divinely-inspired mirrors—helps us become people who truly love God himself, and not just the feelings or things God may graciously give us.

So why do we pray? You'll need to answer that question for yourself, but as for me, I'm learning to pray so that I'll be able to see and know God more and more. That's my heart-felt desire as I journey with the Psalms. I hope it will be your desire as well.

But speaking of journeys, it's time to take the dog out for another walk. Come with me, won't you?

---

12. Towns, *Praying the Psalms*, 11.

Chapter 2

The Psalms and Walking the Dog

> *"The Lord is my shepherd;*
> *I have everything I need.*
> *He lets me rest in green meadows;*
> *he leads me beside peaceful streams.*
> *He renews my strength.*
> *He guides me along right paths,*
> *bringing honor to his name."*

—Psalm 23:1–3 *(New Living Translation)*

The Spiritual Practice of Prayer-Walking

When I was a rookie pastor, I attended a conference in Baltimore with a church elder named Bob. We went there to learn how to establish a certain caregiving program in our church. The conference was both informative and inspirational, and later we did start the program back at our church. When the conference ended, Bob and I climbed into the car for the long drive back to Michigan. I took the first shift at the wheel, and as I steered the car onto the freeway, I said to Bob, "Why don't we take a few minutes and pray for God's blessing as we move ahead with this new program?"

"Okaaay," Bob replied, but I could hear a hint of hesitation in his voice. I figured that wasn't especially unusual, since many people feel a little uncomfortable praying out loud with others. I thought that might well explain Bob's apparent reluctance. But I was the pastor after all, so I decided I should lead off in praying, and I did.

After I had prayed for a few moments, I glanced over at Bob. And then I understood the real reason for his hesitancy. Bob was looking at me very intently—making sure I had my eyes open and on the road while I was praying. I think he wondered if this young pastor could pray and drive at the same time!

That was a funny moment, and we had a good laugh together when we realized what was going on. But that incident shows how engrained we are when it comes to many things—including the ways we pray. For some of us, we're accustomed to always use the same ritual for a meal-time blessing or when we tuck our kids into bed. Or we have a special place where we sit to do our devotions and pray. Or when someone says, "Let's pray . . . ," we automatically clasp our hands, bow our heads, and close our eyes.

Extra Steps:

What are some of your prayer habits? Do you pray at particular times or places? What ways of praying have been especially meaningful to you?

My work with the Psalms has helped me break free from some of my old prayer habits and has led me to embrace some new practices. I want to tell you about one of those in this chapter: *prayer-walking*. Over the years I've prayed in numerous ways. And I've always enjoyed walking (including walking the dog). From time to time I've even prayed while I was walking. But prayer-walking as a spiritual practice is relatively new for me. Yet I didn't just wake up one morning and decide to try prayer-walking as a different way to pray. Rather, my practice of prayer-walking developed gradually over a period of several months. Here's how it came about.

When I settled on Psalm 145 as the text for the sermon I described in the last chapter, I also decided to memorize it. Psalm 145 is a beautiful praise psalm, and I figured that memorizing it would enable me to praise God more. So that's what I did. Over the next couple of weeks, I memorized Psalm 145 while my dog, Emma, and I went on our regular walks. (I'll tell you more about that in the next chapter.) After I had memorized the psalm, I continued to recite it during at least one of those dog walks each day. In that way, the psalm became a daily prayer for me, and I found it was, indeed, a wonderful way to praise God. After all, I was praising God with the very words God had inspired the psalmist to use in praising God.

Since then, I've continued to use my dog-walking times to learn new psalms and to rehearse and pray the old ones. As I've done that, those walks have turned into "prayer walks." As Emma and I walk along, I recite psalms and consciously direct my thoughts toward God. I imagine myself being in a conversation with God, as I reflect on what the psalms teach me about God, as I give thanks to God for his goodness and blessings, and as I listen for the gentle murmurings of God's Spirit. It's been fun to do, and it's led to a renewed growth in my prayer life.

Long ago, Clement of Alexandria described prayer as "keeping company with God." The awareness that I'm walking in "company with God" is what transforms those dog walks into prayer walks. Walking the dog used to be just another necessary chore. Now those dog walks provide me with the opportunity to keep company with God by praying as I walk. I imagine those walks being similar in some mysterious way to the walks Adam and Eve must have enjoyed with God in the Garden of Eden prior to the Fall. I even wonder if perhaps they might have had a dog or two accompanying them on those walks with God. Seems likely to me!

Perhaps praying-while-walking seems as strange to you as praying-while-driving did to Bob. But let's think about this for a moment. Many of our prayer habits were shaped when we were very young. As children, we were most likely taught that the proper posture for prayer is sitting in a chair or a pew, with our hands clasped, head bowed, and eyes closed. As adults, we usually continue to pray that way in worship services, before meals, with someone in the hospital, or at special events. Since we can't imagine walking with our hands clasped, head bowed, and eyes closed, we don't usually associate praying and walking.

But walking while we pray actually has several advantages. For one, it helps us concentrate and pray for more extended periods of time. Personally, I find it very difficult to sit and pray for any length of time. My body gets stiff. I get bored. My mind wanders. Thus, that kind of prayer session usually comes to an end very quickly for me. John Ortberg refers to this as "Spiritual Attention Deficit Disorder."[1] I'm pretty sure I have an acute case of SADD! However, walking keeps me alert and awake, as the exercise moves a little extra oxygen to my brain. The result is that prayer walks enable me to be in conversation with God for much longer periods of time than I ever could in a pew or in my study.

---

1. Ortberg, *Life*, 101.

Another advantage I've discovered is that being outdoors allows God to use nature to speak to me in special ways. On numerous early-morning walks, I've observed a beautiful sunrise and my thoughts have immediately turned to the opening verses of Psalm 8, "Lord, our Lord, how majestic is your name in all the earth! You have set your glory in the heavens." Or when I've seen deer in a nearby field or wild turkeys crossing the street or birds soaring through the sky, I recall, "How many are your works, Lord! In wisdom you made them all; the earth is full of your creatures!" (Ps. 104:24). And I can never pray Psalm 1—especially the phrase, "That person is like a tree planted by streams of water"—without looking up at the towering ponderosa pine trees where I now live. As I walk, I make it a point to notice the world around me—the world that the Lord, the Maker of heaven and earth, has so carefully fashioned. And that leads to praise and worship of the Creator. I'd miss that if all my praying were in a study or a sanctuary.

David Hansen has written a helpful book about prayer-walking entitled *Long Wandering Prayer: An Invitation To Walk with God*. Much of what he's written about "long wandering prayer" echoes my own experience in prayer-walking. For instance, he also describes how walking enables us to pray for longer periods and notes the advantage of praying outdoors, pointing out that "Elijah didn't hear the still small voice in a library."[2] Indeed, we might add that on many of the occasions when the Gospels report Jesus praying, he was also doing so outdoors.

Hansen, however, also provides a theological rationale for why the body is also a part of prayer. He points out that, while prayer is certainly a spiritual activity, that doesn't mean the physical world is irrelevant to the act of praying. We're whole persons—body, mind, soul, and spirit—and our body and brain (our physical self) are as essential for praying as our spirit and soul are. He points out that "we cannot pray a minute longer than our body allows us" and that "when the body falls asleep, praying stops." So he concludes, "We pray body and soul and no other way."[3]

That's certainly true from my own experience with praying. I've read about great spiritual giants who prayed on their knees for hours, but I can't pray that way for more than a couple of minutes. My knees get sore and my legs cramp up, and quickly I'm fidgeting and shifting around trying to get comfortable. It's rather hard to focus on praying while my body's in pain. So even though prayer is communing with God in my spirit, I can't

---

2. Hansen, *Long Wandering Prayer*, 30.
3. Hansen, *Long Wandering Prayer*, 48–50.

separate the physical (my body and my brain) from the spiritual (the act of praying). Prayer-walking simply reflects that fact of life. We sometimes walk to clear our minds or to think through something going on in our life. Why not walk in order to pray?

In her book, *The Power of Listening*, Lynne Baab describes her experience in walking a labyrinth at a cathedral in San Francisco. The exercise helped her to find a deep sense of peace about a major transition in her life. Reflecting on the experience, she noted the significance of the physical act of walking as an aid for the spiritual act of listening to God. She writes, "Sometimes our bodies—as we walk, kneel, garden, or do some other physical activity—open the ears of our heart to hear God's voice or the Holy Spirit's nudges."[4]

According to Calvin Miller, the spiritual practice of prayer-walking hearkens back to the ancient Celtic Christians, who were known as *peregrini pro Christi*, or "wanderers for Christ." He cites in particular the story of a sixth-century Celt named Brendan, who spent his life sailing throughout the Hebrides in western Scotland. Brendan's adventures at sea were merely the setting for his pilgrimage with Christ, however, and his sailing was a way for him to grow closer to Christ.[5] Miller notes that many of those early Celts, like Brendan, were on a pilgrimage through life, both figuratively and literally. They were

> wandering pilgrims who journeyed not to particular shrines or destinations. They spent their lives in worship and ministry as exiles and aliens and strangers. They prayed as they journeyed, always thanking God for the day and asking him to reveal his will for the land on which they traversed. Coupling prayer with trekking, they took part in what today's pilgrims might call "prayer walking."[6]

So it wasn't just that they prayed from time to time (or even prayed a lot) as they traveled. For these *peregrini* the entire journey was a prayer,

---

4. Baab, *Power of Listening*, 26.

5. Miller, *Celtic Prayer*, 74–75. According to Miller, "Celts have often been called the first Europeans or European aborigines. The word *Celt* is from the Greek (*keltos*) and can be translated 'alien' or 'stranger.' Exactly when or where the Celts came from has fostered a long anthropological debate. Some scholars place their beginnings as far back as 1500 B.C. Others say they came from no further back than 500 B.C. Some believe they had their origin in the regions north of India, while others think they were middle European. ... We know for sure that Celtic tribes were in England long before the Saxon and Angles arrived to give it the modern name of 'Angle Land' or England" (*Celtic Prayer*, 8).

6. Miller, *Celtic Prayer*, 25.

because they saw themselves as traveling in the presence of God. That's the essence of long, wandering prayer, as Miller sees it. He writes, "The fullest definition of long, wandering prayer is journeying in the presence of the triune God."[7] This is why Miller can describe his own commutes to and from work in his car as a kind of long, wandering prayer. He explains:

> Whether we talk or listen to God, we are to live in the lifelong abundance of his presence. This sort of presence is the bedrock of long, wandering prayer. This is why my long trek to work and back is fulfilling. God and I are not always in verbal contact, but his presence is real. Thus I am able to define my morning commute as a long, wandering prayer.[8]

My own practice of prayer-walking is similar to Calvin Miller's commutes in his car—and a distant cousin perhaps to Brendan's seafaring. As I walk the dog, I see myself as walking in God's presence. Sometimes I'm talking to God, reciting a psalm or offering another kind of prayer. Sometimes I'm just walking along silently, listening for the murmur of God's Spirit. Sometimes I'm observing something around me or even talking to the dog. But the entire walk is a prayer, because I'm intentionally walking in the company of God. Calvin Miller and David Hansen refer to that as "long, wandering prayer." For me, it's simply "prayer-walking."

I was on one of those prayer walks when it struck me how much Emma is caught up in a world to which I'm largely oblivious. That's the world of scents and smells. She trots along with her nose glued to the ground, zig-zagging back-and-forth as she follows invisible odors. Frequently, she'll stop to give special attention to a clump of grass or a bush or a fencepost. From time to time, her head pops up, and she scans the area, searching for the source of some new smell the breeze has brought her way. That's how she "observes" all those different scents and smells. I, on the other hand, notice the various fragrances around me only occasionally. That's because, like most humans, my world is primarily a visual world. My world is shaped by sight, and my eyes provide most of my sensory input. Thus, Emma and I can be on the same trail, and in the same general space, yet be in two very different worlds.

In a similar way, most people meander through life unmindful of the spiritual world and the presence of God all around them. Sometimes, they'll get brief reminders of God's presence, but mostly they live in the physical

---

7. Miller, *Celtic Prayer*, 79.
8. Miller, *Celtic Prayer*, 79.

world, the world that can be seen, touched, and felt. They're no more aware of God's world than I am of Emma's invisible world. Fortunately, it's easier to become aware of the spiritual world than it is to "see" Emma's world of scents and smells (as fascinating as that might be). And prayer walks help us to do that. As we engage in prayer walks, we learn to walk in God's world, listening for God's Spirit and becoming more attuned to God's presence.

That's why I refer to these prayer walks as "holy walks." The word "holy" doesn't mean "religious," or even "sacred." It basically means "set apart." Something is "holy" when it's been set apart, or dedicated, for a special purpose. For instance, those special dishes you only use when guests come over for dinner? They could be described as "holy dishes." What makes the holy walks described in this book holy is their special purpose: they're times for us to intentionally walk with God—even if we're also walking the dog, or getting a little exercise, or enjoying some fresh air. My dog walks with Emma become holy walks whenever I turn them into prayer walks, keeping company with God and seeking to walk in God's world. That's the purpose behind this spiritual practice of prayer-walking, whether we're sailing the seas with Brendan, commuting to work in our car like Calvin Miller, or walking our dog through the neighborhood. We're learning to walk in God's world.

On a side note, when I wrote this chapter, I wrestled with what to call "prayer-walking" (and "heart-learning" in the next chapter). *Spiritual discipline* is the common term for such activities. However, I've chosen instead to refer to the activities described in this book as *spiritual practices*. To me, "discipline" implies that I've achieved a certain level of proficiency, while "practice" acknowledges that I am still very much a learner. In my mind, spiritual disciplines are for people who are far more proficient than I. So I'll stick with "spiritual practices" and keep on trying to get better at them. Maybe one day they'll become spiritual disciplines for me. So, spiritual practice or spiritual discipline? I'll leave that call up to you.

Prayer-Walking and the Psalms of Ascent

In biblical times, God's people generally prayed while standing up, perhaps because it would have been viewed as improper to be seated in the presence of someone important, like a king—or like God. Standing was a sign of respect. In addition, when people were in great anguish, they might prostrate themselves—lie flat on the ground—which is an incredibly humble and vulnerable position. That might befit someone who feels themselves to be in great need.

But we can also be confident that God's people talked to God while they were walking. Hansen points out that the Hebrews developed their prayer tradition long before they had a temple, and he observes the impact their lifestyle had on their prayers: "From Abraham to David, the Hebrews were a shepherding, moving folk. They lived out-of-doors easily, though not painlessly. Following the scent of green pastures, they passed through death valleys, ascended passes and crossed rivers. Wandering lay at the core of their psyche from the beginning, and it shaped their life with God."[9]

Praying outdoors, while walking, was simply a way of life for God's people of long ago. They didn't just jump in a car and drive to wherever they needed to go. They walked. Sometimes they walked for hours or even days to get someplace. And during those long treks, their thoughts would frequently turn to the One they loved and followed. In fact, there's a collection of fifteen psalms that quite likely were written especially for people to use as they were traveling. They're often called the *Psalms of Ascent*, and they have much to teach us about walking and praying.

The Psalms of Ascent are numbered 120–134 in God's Prayer Book. According to Thomas Merton, "Perhaps these short, joyful songs are the most beautiful in the whole Psalter. They are full of light and confidence. They bring God very close to us."[10] Scholars aren't certain of the purpose for this collection of psalms. However, most commentators interpret them in light of the tradition which holds that they were sung or recited by pilgrims traveling to Jerusalem for the three annual feasts that were commanded in Exodus 34:18–23:

- The Feast of Unleavened Bread (also called the Feast of Passover, it commemorated the Hebrews' deliverance from Egypt and was held in the spring)
- The Feast of Weeks (or the Feast of Pentecost, which commemorated the entry into the Promised Land and also celebrated the wheat harvest; it was held in the early summer)
- The Feast of Tabernacles (which celebrated the ingathering in the fall as well as the beginning of the new year)

---

9. Hansen, *Long Wandering Prayer*, 43.
10. Merton, *Praying the Psalms*, 31.

The Jews were a people used to long journeys (think Egypt, Exodus, and Wilderness), and the more devout ones made the journey to Jerusalem for these festivals three times a year. As they traveled, the Psalms of Ascent would have reminded them of the reasons they were making the trip to Jerusalem once again. They would have recalled that they were God's covenant people. They would have remembered the many ways God had rescued his people in the past and how God had promised to deliver them in the future as well. They would have been celebrating the opportunity to go to Jerusalem once again to worship this merciful, loving, covenant-keeping God who delivers his people again and again. Singing and reciting the Psalms of Ascent would have been an act of worship in itself, as the pilgrims prepared their hearts to celebrate the great festivals in the Holy City.

In prayer-walking, we're not traveling to Jerusalem, of course. In fact, we may not be going any place in particular. Quite likely, we're simply walking around the neighborhood or through a park. However, I believe our prayer walks today are actually quite similar to those early pilgrimages the Jews made to Jerusalem. Prayer walks are a daily reminder that the entire Christian life is a journey. And when the Psalms are a part of our prayer walks, we're following in the footsteps of those ancient people of God who prayed the Psalms of Ascent during their travels to Jerusalem.[11] In his book, *A Long Obedience in the Same Direction*, Eugene Peterson makes this observation about the Psalms of Ascent:

> There are no better "songs for the road" for those who travel the way of faith in Christ, a way that has so many continuities with the way of Israel. Since many (not all) essential items in Christian discipleship are incorporated in these songs, they provide a way to remember who we are and where we are going.[12]

He adds that when we learn to sing these songs well, when we learn to pray the Psalms well, they become a kind of handbook or guidebook for our daily walk with Christ.

The first Psalm of Ascent that I memorized is Psalm 121, and it's still one of my favorites. To help you appreciate this psalm, I'd like to guide you through a short exercise. Don't read the psalm just yet. Instead, if you're able, stand up and imagine that you're one of those pilgrims making the long walk to Jerusalem. The Holy City sits on top of a small hill. It isn't especially

---

11. Thomas Merton says that "St. Augustine calls [the Psalms of Ascent] the Psalms of our journey to the heavenly Jerusalem" (*Praying the Psalms*, 31).

12. Peterson, *A Long Obedience*, 15.

high, but it *is* the highest city around and requires a long ascent in order to reach it. So you're looking *up* at the city as you walk. Although you can't see the temple yet, try picturing it in your mind. You know it's in the center of the city, and it's your ultimate destination.

If you really want to get into it, start walking around the room. As you walk, keep in mind that there are no paved bike paths, no sidewalks. You're walking on a dusty, rocky road. *Watch out! Don't stumble!* It's also very hot, and you've been walking for many hours. Can you feel the sun baking down on you? The sweat running down your face? Your clothes sticking to your skin? You've come a long way and you're tired. Perhaps you even spent last night camped out by the road—no Holiday Inns along this route.

Can you imagine that journey? What are you thinking as you walk along?

Now take out your Bible and read Psalm 121 (or have someone read it to you) while you're walking around the room. Read it aloud, slowly, and notice the words and phrases that stand out to you. You may want to read it three or four times as you walk. Let the words sink into your heart as they become more and more familiar.

* * *

What did you hear in the psalm? Perhaps you've heard or read this psalm before. How did being on a "journey" affect what you noticed in the psalm this time?

I wonder if you heard the repetition of the phrase "watch over" or "watches over"? In the *NIV* it occurs five times in these eight short verses. That phrase shouts to me every time I pray this psalm. How reassuring to know that the Lord is watching over us, even as we travel this dusty, hot, dangerous road to Jerusalem. Or as we drive on a busy road like Division Avenue here in Spokane. Or walk through the quad on campus. Or mosey along the aisles in the grocery store. "The LORD watches over you."

How about the references to time? Did you hear the psalmist speak of "day" and "night" and of "now" and "forevermore"? We take days off, we go on vacations, we take breaks. But God never does. God never slumbers nor sleeps. God watches over us 24/7/365. Even when we're sleeping. Even when we're ignoring him. God is always watching over us. Always.

These pilgrims of old would have often been looking up as they traveled, looking up not only at Jerusalem, but also looking up at the other mountains around them. They weren't sitting in a church sanctuary when they prayed,

"I lift up my eyes to the mountains." The geography and terrain prompted thoughts about God and where their help really came from. Were you looking up as you read those words? Where does your help come from?

If you looked up while you walked and read this psalm, did you also have to glance down to make sure you didn't stumble over anything? When we're looking up, it's all too easy to trip over something we haven't seen. We've all done that on occasion. Yet as we listen to Psalm 121, we hear the words, "He will not let your foot slip." More reassurance for the pilgrim, not just on the journey to Jerusalem but on the journey through life ("now and forevermore").

Psalm 121 is short, but it's certainly a most appropriate psalm for us to pray as part of our walk with the Lord. I took you through the above exercise to help you *feel* the words of the psalm. A psalm truly becomes a prayer when we're able to identify emotionally with its words, thoughts, and feelings. There's an important place for Bible study and biblical research, but simply knowing more *about* a psalm doesn't make it a prayer for us. The psalm needs to become a *part* of us. So take a few moments to read Psalm 121 one more time. Offer it to God as your prayer.

Extra Steps:

As you reflect on Psalm 121, try to imagine yourself as an ancient pilgrim. How might this psalm have encouraged you on your journey to Jerusalem? What encouragement does it give you for your daily journey through life in this day?

Of course, Psalm 121 is but one of the fifteen Psalms of Ascent. If you read through the other fourteen in the collection, you'll notice additional ways that these psalms would be especially appropriate for someone journeying to Jerusalem:

- For instance, Psalm 122, which is one of the four Psalms of Ascent attributed to King David, focuses on prayers for Jerusalem, the City of David. As the pilgrims traveled to Jerusalem, it would be natural to pray for the Holy City, the center of Jewish life for so many centuries.
- Psalm 125 draws upon the geography around Jerusalem in a similar way to Psalm 121. Looking at the mountains that surround the city

and provide natural security for it, the psalmist celebrates the way the Lord surrounds his people and provides protection for them.

- Psalm 127 is attributed to Solomon, who built the first temple in Jerusalem. In this psalm, Solomon refers to the importance of the Lord building and guarding one's house and family. The temple was the primary destination for these pilgrims, and Solomon draws upon his experience in building the temple to teach the people about the Lord's protection and blessing.

- Psalm 130 would have been especially meaningful for those who were traveling to Jerusalem to celebrate one of the great feasts. Anticipating the sacrifices and offerings for sin which they'd be making at the temple, this psalm is a cry for God's mercy and forgiveness. It's also a prayer of great faith and confidence that the Lord "will redeem Israel from all their sins" (v. 8).

The Psalms of Ascent are prayers for people who are on a journey. When we engage in prayer-walking, we're doing what God's people did since the beginning of human history. They walked, and they prayed. And we're walking in their footsteps, with the psalms of God's Prayer Book guiding us along the way. In the next chapter we'll discuss how we can bring the Psalms with us on our prayer walks.

Extra Steps:

On a sheet of notepaper, write out the words to one of the Psalms of Ascent (most of them are relatively short). Then take the sheet with you and go for a walk (outdoors, if possible). Several times during your walk, pause and read the psalm aloud. Be aware of the thoughts that come into your mind as you read it and, later, as you continue to walk along.

Chapter 3

Teaching an Old Dog a New Trick

> *"I have hidden your word in my heart*
> *that I might not sin against you.*
> *Praise be to you, Lord;*
> *teach me your decrees.*
> *With my lips I recount*
> *all the laws that come from your mouth."*
>
> —Psalm 119:11–13

An "Old" Pastor's New "Trick"

A WHILE AGO, I made an effort to teach Emma to shake her paw. She wasn't catching on quite as quickly as I thought she should, and that caused me to wonder if there's truth in the saying that you can't teach an old dog new tricks. You see, at the time Emma was ten years old, which is getting up there in dog years. So I tried to stay patient with her, figuring that this small trick might be a bit of a challenge for her. Since I first started working with her, she's been making some progress. Now she shakes her paw whenever *she* decides to. I'm still working to get her to do it when *I* tell her to.

It may be hard for old dogs to learn new tricks, but this "old" pastor has been working on a new "trick"—and so far I'm learning it pretty well, even if I do say so myself. Plus, I'm having a ball doing it! Let me tell you about it.

When I was preparing the sermon on the alternative to shopping-list prayers (see chapter 1), I chose Psalm 145 as the Scriptural text because it's a wonderful psalm of praise to God. I was planning to teach that our prayers should include more praise to God, and Psalm 145 is a great model for that (I'll say more about this psalm in chapter 8). In line after line the psalmist praises God for his various attributes and actions. As I studied the psalm and reflected on all those reasons to praise God, I decided that I would memorize it.

Now, I hadn't done any serious memorizing of the Bible for a long time, and Psalm 145 is a somewhat lengthy passage (twenty-one verses). But I made up some flash cards, and I began memorizing the verses as I took Emma for her daily walks. It took me three or four weeks, but I stuck with it, and eventually I had it memorized. After that, Psalm 145 became a daily prayer for me. Every time Emma and I made one of our regular journeys around the neighborhood, I recited it as a prayer to God. After a while, something clicked for me. I felt like I was truly praising God in a deeper way than perhaps I had ever done before—and that felt very good and very right.

Little did I realize that was just the beginning. I was on the way to learning a new "trick."

A couple of weeks after I delivered that sermon on Psalm 145, I was visiting with an elderly woman named Gert. At the time, Gert was under hospice care, and she would live for only a few more months. At the end of our visit that particular day, I read Psalm 23 to her. The Shepherd Psalm was one of Gert's favorites, as it is for many of us. However, I didn't read it to her in the *King James Version* that she had grown up with. Instead, I read it to her in the *New Living Translation*, a modern translation that I really like. The fresh wording of the *NLT* appealed to Gert as well, and she asked me to be sure to read it to her again the next time I visited.

Suddenly, a thought popped into my head (I believe it was a nudging from God), and I told Gert that I would memorize the psalm and then recite it to her the next time I saw her. And that's what I did. During Gert's final weeks of earthly life, I often recited that version of Psalm 23 to her as part of our closing prayers together. It was also one of the Scripture passages that we included in her memorial service.

So I had now memorized two psalms. During the following months, I began memorizing other psalms as well. I took on Psalm 8 after I heard Dr. Trygve Johnson, Dean of the Chapel at Hope College, preach on it during a campus worship service called the Gathering. I tackled Psalm 13 after listening to Pastor Frank Thomas preach about it during a worship conference at Calvin College. One of my long-time favorites, Psalm 84, came next. Psalm 100 was another one the Lord drew me to, along with Psalm 19. I decided to memorize Psalm 47 when our church's lead pastor, Judson Marvel, said he was going to preach on it for Ascension Day, and I learned Psalm 95 after we discussed it during one of our church staff meetings. And so on it has gone.

I've now memorized more than forty psalms, so, evidently, this "old" pastor is still very capable of learning a new "trick" or two. But the number of psalms I've learned isn't the point. What matters is that this memory work has caused me to spend a lot of time with the Psalms. And in the process I've fallen in love with the book of Psalms and have discovered a fresh way of praying. So, if you're looking for a way to re-energize your own prayer life, I want to challenge you to give this "trick" a try. You may just find that it will breathe new life into your prayers, as it has mine. In the rest of the chapter, I'll tell you how to do this.

Extra Steps:

What value do you see in memorizing Scripture, especially since we generally forget it when we stop rehearsing what we've learned?

How is memorizing Scripture different from memorizing the state capitals or U.S. presidents, like many of us did back in grade school?

Memorizing or Heart-Learning?

Before we discuss some practical ways to memorize psalms, I want us to consider what we're really doing when we undertake this task. Indeed, is "memorizing" even the proper way to talk about this spiritual practice?

I didn't grow up in the church, so I didn't have a young child's experience of memorizing Bible verses in Sunday School. But when I was in my twenties and thirties, I worked in a ministry with college students. During that time, I memorized quite a few Bible verses. One time, I even spent several months memorizing the New Testament book of 1 John. It was a book I had been studying and wanted to know better. So one day I just decided to do take on the challenge of memorizing it. I ended up getting a nice benefit from doing that.

Shortly after I finished memorizing 1 John, I took a summer course in New Testament Greek as part of my pre-seminary training. It was an intensive course that packed a year's worth of Greek into just four weeks. For various reasons, I had arranged to take the final exam at a different time from the rest of the class. So I went to the professor's office to take the exam, as I'd been told to do. The professor wasn't there, but his secretary gave me a copy of the exam and pointed me to a table where I could work on it. I sat down, nervously opened up the exam, and looked at it. The entire exam consisted of just one assignment. I had to translate a certain, lengthy passage from the New Testament. But guess which New Testament book the passage happened to be in? Right! It was 1 John. Probably the easiest "A" I ever got.

As I've gotten back into memorizing Scripture through my work with the Psalms, I've also been reflecting on what it really means to memorize verses or passages from the Bible. Memorizing any verse or passage in God's Word is a valuable and worthwhile task. But is the memorizing I've done with the Psalms different from when I memorized various verses in the Bible as a young college pastor? Or even from when I memorized the book of 1 John? That's the question I've wrestled with.

My conclusion is that, yes, it is different—and in a very important way. In fact, that difference has led me to describe my memory work with the Psalms as *heart-learning* instead of as memorizing. Let me explain the difference.

Memorizing was always a major part of learning throughout my student days, from kindergarten all the way up through two graduate degrees. Memorizing the alphabet as a first-grader. Memorizing the multiplication table in elementary school. Memorizing the state capitals in a geography class, and the U.S. presidents in social studies. Memorizing the periodic table of elements in high school chemistry. Memorizing a poem or two in English lit classes. Memorizing key points in the psychology experiments I learned about in college. Memorizing important names and dates in church history. You get the idea, and I'm sure you can think of many things you've had to memorize over the years as well.

That kind of memory work, however, was primarily for *information*. In memorizing all those things (and many more like them), I gained knowledge. But that kind of knowledge was aimed at my *head*. It shaped my *mind* so that I could become a more educated person. That's a good thing, of course, but the goal in memorizing Scripture should be more than just producing a more educated Christian. It should be more than simply amassing information about the Bible or acquiring a few inspiring or encouraging verses that we can call to mind—as valuable as that may be. In memorizing passages in the Bible, my desire is that God's Word will shape my *heart* (not just my mind) so that my values, my goals, my attitudes, and even my thoughts, are more in line with God's.

This is why I now refer to memorizing the psalms as heart-learning. Heart-learning takes me beyond rote memory of various words and phrases. In heart-learning I make a conscious choice to allow the words of the psalm to become written on my heart, to allow the thoughts in those words to become the thoughts of my heart. That doesn't happen just by reading a psalm a few times, or even by memorizing it. But when I memorize it and then pray it over and over, the words of the psalm seep into my soul and slowly shape my heart. Of course, this can happen with other passages and books in the Bible as well, but the psalms are especially appropriate for this.

God once described David, the shepherd boy who became king of Israel, as "a man after my own heart" (Acts 13:22). It's no coincidence that David was the author of so many of the psalms. As we heart-learn various psalms, including many that were likely written by David himself, we allow God to shape our hearts so that we, too, can become women and men after God's own heart.

When I've talked with people about heart-learning psalms like this, most agree that it's a valuable practice to undertake, but many also come up with various excuses for why they could never do it.

The most common excuse is a *lack of time*. People often say they don't have the time to memorize or heart-learn a psalm. Time, of course, is a major issue for everyone. That's why I usually combine my psalms work with walking the dog. After all, Emma needs to go out on a regular basis, which gives me ample opportunities to learn and pray the Psalms. Every day God gives us contains 1,440 minutes, but we get to decide how to use all those minutes. It may take some creativity, but if you can find ten minutes two or three times a day, you have the time to learn a psalm (and multiple psalms as well). So most of us can overcome the time obstacle if we choose to do so.

In addition to time, another excuse I hear quite often is *age*. Far too many people tell me, "I'm too old to memorize Bible passages." But that simply isn't true. As we get older, it does take longer to learn new things, so we need to be patient with ourselves. And some of us are undoubtedly better than others at memorizing things, just as some of us are better at math, or writing, or woodworking, or just about any skill. But, unless you have some kind of dementia or mental disability, age alone will not prevent you from heart-learning a psalm. We *can* learn new things no matter how old we get.

I have an aunt who will always be my hero in this regard. Aunt Kate first learned to use a computer when she was 80 years old. She's a smart lady, but she didn't learn to do email and word processing just because she's so intelligent. No, she had the right attitude, she got some assistance (she hired a young man to tutor her when she got her first computer), and she stayed patient with herself through the time it took to learn it. When she turned 100 a few years ago, she was still using her computer. I often tell people, "If my Aunt Kate can learn to use a Mac when she's 80 years old, you can heart-learn a psalm or two (or three or four)."

Extra Steps:

What previous experiences (good or bad) have you had in memorizing Scripture?

Do you recall ever memorizing any of the psalms? If so, which ones? (Special bonus: Can you still recite them?)

What are your feelings about memorizing Scripture at the present time? What difference, if any, do you think it makes to view the task as "heart-learning" instead of simply "memorizing"?

Do you see your time or age as major barriers to heart-learning psalms? If you do, how might you overcome those obstacles?

How To Heart-Learn a Psalm

If you're still reading this chapter, I hope it means you've decided to try heart-learning a psalm or two with me. Congratulations! I think you've made a great choice, and I know you'll be blessed by God as you take on this challenge. If you're well-experienced in memorizing Bible verses, keep on using whatever method works for you. But if this is a new adventure for you, you might consider using some of the approaches and techniques that I use. Here's how I go about memorizing (or heart-learning) a new psalm:

1. The first step is to *select the psalm*. I like to have a sense that I've heard God's voice in the Scripture passages I learn. When we recognize a particular psalm as being especially meaningful and appropriate for us, Thomas Merton says that "is an actual grace of God."[1] He goes on to explain that that's the Spirit's way of urging us to focus on those psalms and incorporate them into our own prayers and meditations. So choose a psalm that's been especially meaningful to you, one that God has used to encourage, comfort, or inspire you. For your first psalm, I suggest you begin with a relatively short one, such as Psalm 1, 23, 100, or 121. That will give you a sense of accomplishment very quickly and can serve as a motivation to take on a second one. Once you select the psalm, remember that this is God's Word, and God's Word always accomplishes what God wants it to accomplish (see Isaiah 55:11). So ask God to work in your heart as you learn the psalm.

2. Next, *choose the translation* in which to memorize the psalm. John Witvliet urges us to be students of multiple translations and paraphrases because of "the nuance and intensity of the poetry of the Psalms."[2] To make his point, he discusses Psalm 42:1–2 in several translations and shows the strengths and weaknesses of each rendition. He cautions us about choosing a version simply because it happens to say what we want it to say, but he also says we mustn't limit ourselves to the version we're most accustomed to.

    For most of my biblical work, I use the *New International Version*, because that's the version that's used in the churches I've served. This popular translation was thoroughly updated in 2011, and I find it to be clear, contemporary, and generally pleasing to the ear. But from time to time I've chosen other versions for particular psalms. For example, I mentioned using the *New Living Translation* for Psalm 23. I also used that version for Psalm 25. But I learned Psalm 98 in the *English Standard Version* and Psalm 134 in the *New Revised Standard Version*. In these other cases, I simply preferred the phrasing of those translations over that in the *NIV*.

    The web site I use most often for exploring different translations of the Bible is www.BibleGateway.com, which is especially good on my laptop. YouVersion is the Bible app I use most often on my smartphone. It's free, and it also allows you to download versions of the

---

1. Merton, *Praying the Psalms*, 26–27.
2. Witvliet, *Psalms in Christian Worship*, 62.

Bible to your phone so you can read it even if you're in an area without Internet or wireless access (most of those versions are free as well). It also offers numerous Bible reading plans and other helpful materials. You can find that at www.YouVersion.com or www.Bible.com.

So before you begin memorizing your psalm, read it in several translations and pay attention to the differences. Does one of them seem to speak to you more powerfully than the others, and, if so, why? Choose the version that speaks most clearly to you.

3. Once you've selected your psalm and the translation, make up *flash cards* to assist with the memory work. You can purchase a pack of 4" x 6" plain note cards and cut individual cards into a convenient 1½" x 4" size (yielding four flash cards from each note card). Write out a verse or two on one side of the flash card and the Scripture reference on the other. Make up as many flash cards as you need for the entire psalm. Here's what your cards might look like:

Psalm 134:1-3 (NRSV)

Front of flash card

---

¹ Come, bless the Lord, all you servants of the Lord,
  who stand by night in the house of the Lord.

² Lift up your hands to the holy place,
  and bless the Lord.

³ May the Lord, Maker of heaven and earth, bless you from Zion.

Back of flash card

The advantage of using flash cards is that you can easily carry them with you on your prayer-walks, or to work or school or other places. They slip easily into a pocket or a purse, and you can review them almost any place when you get a few minutes.

4. *Repetition* is the most basic tool in the memorizing process, and there's simply no way to avoid it. So, start by reading a verse (or part of a verse) on your flashcard. Then turn the card over and try to recite it without looking. Then turn it back over and check yourself. Then repeat the process: read it, turn it over, recite it from memory, and check yourself. Continue doing that until you can recite the entire card word for word without looking at it. It may take you a few sessions before you can reliably do that, but keep at it. Once you begin to have one flashcard down, start on the next one. As you get the second one memorized, be sure to keep reciting the first flashcard as well. Keep doing that until you have the entire psalm memorized.

5. As you review your flashcards over and over, *speak out loud* and *get your body involved* by walking and gesturing. At first it may feel weird to say the psalm out loud, but this is actually a critical part in heart-learning. When you hear the words as well as think them, and when you get your body involved as well, the words begin to permeate your whole being and not just your mind. So raise your hands when the psalm calls for that, or lift up your eyes. And if you worry about people seeing you talking to yourself, just get a blue-tooth device for your ear, and they'll think you're talking on a smartphone. You'll be the only one who knows you're actually on speed-dial with God!

6. Another key is to *recite the psalm frequently*, rather than relying on fewer-but-longer time blocks. When you're learning a psalm, spending ten minutes three times during a day will be much more productive than one thirty-minute session. Incidentally, if you do it that way, you'll also be following the traditional Jewish pattern of praying three times a day. The New Testament scholar, Joachim Jeremias, notes that Jesus himself would have followed this practice: "No day in the life of Jesus passed without the three times of prayer: the morning prayer at sunrise, the afternoon prayer at the time when the afternoon sacrifice was offered in the Temple, the evening prayer at night before going to sleep."[3] Once you get the psalm memorized, you can continue to

---

3. Quoted by Sire, *Learning To Pray*, 212.

review it at various times throughout the day—even while you're waiting for a traffic light.

7. As you recite the psalm, *work at understanding* what you're saying. This is essential! Don't just memorize words, but strive to recite the psalm with feeling and meaning. Your goal should be for the words of the psalm to become *your* words. So constantly ask yourself questions like: *Why did the psalmist say this? What did he mean by that expression? What may have been going on in his life when he prayed these words?* You might want to read what a commentary says about the psalm as well. The more you understand the psalm, the easier it will be to learn it.

    Thomas Merton expresses the kind of attitude we should bring to the heart-learning task when he writes, "No matter whether we understand a Psalm at first or not, we should take it up with this end in view: to make use of it as a prayer that will *enable us to surrender ourselves to God*."[4] So even when you don't fully understand a psalm, you can still make it your prayer. Then your understanding will grow as you continue to recite the psalm. On many occasions I've wondered about the way a psalmist expressed some thought or why he made a certain transition. And, frequently, after days or even weeks of praying the psalm, I'll begin to understand what I think the psalmist meant. I take that as an indication I'm beginning to think like the psalmist. The psalm is becoming more and more a part of my heart. I'm moving from simple memorizing to heart-learning.

8. It's also important to *visualize* what's being described in the verse or passage. I'll talk more about the use of imagery in the book of Psalms in chapter 5, but this is part of understanding the psalm. For instance, Psalm 1 refers to a tree. That's easy to picture in our mind. But how about the temple? Can you visualize that? Or a mountain? Or a fortress? You might even consider drawing simple pictures to help the images stick in your mind.

9. Strive to *memorize the passage exactly*, word for word, just as you find it in the translation you chose. This may seem to make the task more difficult, but I think you'll discover this is actually easier than saying it in slightly different ways each time you recite it. Even when you think you've learned a psalm, you'll have those occasional "brain cramps"

---

4. Merton, *Praying the Psalms*, 26 (emphasis his).

when you forget a word or mix up a phrase. When that happens, simply go back to your flash cards and review that part of the psalm a few extra times. That will solidify the psalm even more in your memory.

10. On occasion, it may be helpful to look for *acronyms* in the psalm you're learning. A while ago I watched an on-line video of Dr. Tim Brown, president of Western Theological Seminary, as he taught a group of students about memorizing Scripture. He used Psalm 134 for the exercise and pointed out the acronym CALM as an aid for remembering that psalm:

Come, bless the Lord,

All you servants of the Lord, who stand by night in the house of the Lord.

Lift up your hands to the holy place, and bless the Lord.

May the Lord, maker of heaven and earth, bless you from Zion.

I've formatted the psalm in a different way from what you'll find in the *New Revised Standard Version* in order to highlight this acronym. Admittedly, this is a very short psalm (just three verses), but Dr. Brown had the class learn it in just twenty minutes, in part by using this technique. I memorized it right along with the class while I watched the video. (Dr. Brown also demonstrates how to visualize the psalm by drawing stick figures. If you have an artistic bent, you may find that approach to be helpful. Check out the video.[5])

Of course, acronyms such as CALM are simply our own inventions to aid in the memorizing task. They're not God-inspired in any way. When I was memorizing a passage in the Apostle Paul's letter to the Philippians on another occasion, I was having a hard time remembering the order of the phrases, "whatever is true, whatever is noble, whatever is right, whatever is pure, whatever is lovely, whatever is admirable" (Phil. 4:8). The phrases seemed completely random. Then I made up a silly sentence to use as an acronym: "True Natives Rightfully Protect Lovely Assets." I'll let you figure out how the words of that weird sentence line up with Paul's words. I know it's a pretty crazy acronym, but it's worked for me. Now I never forget the order of those phrases. So go ahead and invent as many acronyms as you wish.

---

5. You can view the video at http://vimeo.com/53013128.

11. As you heart-learn *additional psalms*, continue to review the ones you've learned previously. For a long time, I would recite all the psalms I had learned every day. I might vary the order, and I didn't pray through all of them on every walk. But in the course of two or three walks each day I was able to review all of them on a daily basis. I'm now at a point where I can no longer do that because of the time it would require. What has worked well for me now is that I recite my three or four newest psalms every day and then rotate through the other psalms as time permits. However, I make sure that I pray through every psalm I've learned at least once every few weeks. That keeps them sharp and fresh in my mind and in my heart.

* * *

Not so difficult, is it? I have all the confidence that you can do it—*if* you're willing to make the commitment and put in some effort and practice. But, of course, that's true about learning anything new. Think back to a time when you developed some new skill. Perhaps you learned to play a musical instrument, or tackled a new subject in school, or picked up a new task at work, or learned a second (or third) language, or started a new hobby. Whatever it was, learning something new required some time and some work, didn't it?

I remember learning that lesson when I was playing on my high school's basketball team. At the time, I lived for basketball, and I wanted to do everything I could to become a better basketball player. I attended a summer basketball camp so that I could learn some new skills and practice against really good players. (This was long before AAU travel teams or year-round sports programming existed.) I also attempted to put on some weight by drinking special protein milkshakes. (I was skinny as a beanstalk in those days; today I have no problem putting on extra weight.) And one summer I decided I would become a better free throw shooter by shooting at least 100 free throws every day until school started back up in the fall.

My dad had installed a hoop and backboard on the roof overhanging our driveway. I carefully measured fifteen feet out from the backboard and painted a free throw line on the driveway. And nearly every day that summer, I went out there by myself and shot 100 free throws. I kept a chart, and each day I recorded how many I had made. On those days when the weather didn't allow me to get outside to do my shooting, I made up for it by shooting 200 free throws the next day.

My practice that summer paid off. I became the best free throw shooter on my team that season and shot better than 80 percent in our games. Even today, all these years later, I could probably beat many NBA players in a free throw contest. The lesson is this: If we want to learn something badly enough, and if we practice enough, and if we practice in the right way, we *will* learn it.

And that's true with memorizing psalms as well.

Ben Patterson certainly understands this. Patterson is the chaplain at Westmont College in Santa Barbara, California. He's also been a longtime champion for memorizing Scripture and has committed several entire books of the Bible to memory (including Romans and Revelation). Here's what he writes about memorizing psalms:

> Memorize the Psalms—but not by rote. Rather, learn them by heart; make their words your words. Come to understand them so well you can recite them—by inflection and tone—as though you had written them yourself. This is, by far, the best way I know to learn to pray the Psalms. I can think of no more powerful way to allow the Word of God to change who you are and how you think.[6]

Patterson doesn't use the term "heart-learning," but this is clearly the direction he's going when he talks about allowing the Word of God to change us. One can memorize a psalm (perhaps for a class on poetry or creative writing) without allowing it into one's heart. But when we memorize a psalm in the way Patterson describes (and the way I've described in the this chapter), we move beyond simple memorizing and into heart-learning. And that will make all the difference.

So how about it? I'm planning to keep on learning more psalms, even at my "old" age, and I'm also going to keep trying to teach Emma to shake her paw. I figure if I can heart-learn all these psalms, surely she can learn to shake her paw. After all, even old dogs can learn new tricks, can't they?

Extra Steps:

What benefits would you see for yourself if you were to heart-learn some of the psalms?

What factors might make this difficult for you and how might you overcome those challenges?

---

6. Patterson, *God's Prayer Book*, 21.

Chapter 4

A Walking Conversation

*"I call out to the L*ORD*,*

and he answers me from his holy mountain."

—P SALM 3:4

THIS MORNING EMMA AND I walked in the nature preserve near our home. That's one of our favorite places to walk, and the weather today was perfect. At one point I stopped to chat with two friends we encountered on the trail, and, on several occasions, Emma got to "chat" with a couple of her dog friends as well. In and around that bit of socializing, I also had a conversation with God.

Now, this wasn't the first conversation I've had with God. In fact, I view each of the holy walks Emma and I go on as being a conversation with God. After all, prayer isn't a speech; it's a *dialogue*. I've always believed that. Prayer is so much more than just me talking to God.

Yet, much of the time those prayer-conversations seem rather one-sided: I talk to God far more than I listen to him. As a modern-day monk once observed, "Samuel said, 'Speak, Lord, for Thy servant is listening'; we more often say, 'Listen, Lord, for Thy servant is speaking.'"[1] When I first came across that quotation, I thought, "Ouch!" because that's all too accurate when it comes to the prayer life of *this* servant of the Lord.

But my practice of prayer-walking and praying the Psalms has been teaching me to listen for God's voice more often while I pray. As I pray through various psalms on these holy walks, I do a lot of speaking—probably still way too much—but I'm also learning to keep my spiritual ears

---

1. Okholm, *Monk Habits*, 38.

open. I'm trying to listen more in case God does want to speak or say something to me.

This morning was one of those times. As I was praying Psalm 32, God's Spirit spoke to me very clearly. It wasn't an audible voice, like Samuel heard that night in the temple, but I heard God nonetheless. Let me explain.

There's a phrase in Psalm 32 that I had never really understood. I memorized this psalm a while ago, but the end of verse 2 had never made much sense to me. The entire verse reads, "Blessed is the one whose sin the LORD does not count against them and in whose spirit is no deceit." The phrase that perplexed me was "in whose spirit is no deceit." I wondered, *Why "deceit"?* Why not anger, or pride, or lust, or some other sin? Why single out deceit when there are so many other sins that inhabit our spirits?

Earlier this morning, before Emma and I went for our walk, I happened to read the chapter on "Humility" in Dennis Okholm's book, *Monk Habits for Everyday People*. The book is organized around themes from *The Rule of St. Benedict*, and in this chapter Okholm explains that true humility involves "radical self-honesty."[2] In other words, growth in spiritual maturity requires that we know ourselves more and more and that we're completely honest with ourselves about both our faults and our strengths.

This morning as I prayed through Psalm 32, the Spirit put that teaching about self-honesty together with that troublesome phrase in verse 2. For the first time I realized the psalmist wasn't talking about lying to someone or deceiving another person in some way. No, the psalmist was talking about *self*-deceit, about deceiving *oneself*. The verse is saying that I will be blessed when I have no self-deception in me. When I can be fully honest with myself about my sin, then I can confess it to God, accept God's forgiveness, and allow God's grace to work in that area. That's what Psalm 32 is really all about, and this morning I came to understand that in a deeper way than I ever had before.

You probably already understood the meaning of that phrase, since I look at it now and wonder why it had been so baffling for me. But, for me, this was an example of the Holy Spirit guiding me into all truth, as Jesus promised the Spirit would do for his followers (John 16:13). It was as though the Spirit said, "You know, Steve, here's what that phrase you've wondered about really means. . . ." Then, afterwards, I spent several minutes "conversing" with the Spirit about the insight I'd been given. *How well do I really know myself? In what ways am I deceiving myself about who I am, about my personal strengths,*

---

2. Okholm, *Monk Habits*, 69.

and about my weaknesses? I suspect this morning's conversation with the Lord won't be the last one we'll have about that topic.

In his insightful book, *Hearing God*, Dallas Willard writes that "people are meant to live in an ongoing conversation with God, speaking and being spoken to."[3] Indeed, *Hearing God* is subtitled "Developing a Conversational Relationship with God." One implication of this conversational nature of our relationship with God is that God desires that our holy walks become "walking conversations." Most of this book focuses on how we speak to God by praying the words of the Psalms, but in this chapter I'll explore these "walking conversations" from both sides of the dialogue. In the first section I'll discuss the specific issue of how we address God. Then in the second section, I'll look at how we hear God's voice, how we can learn to listen for God's voice as we pray the Psalms.

Addressing God in the Psalms

Since God's Prayer Book is intended to teach us how to pray, we can reasonably expect the Psalms to teach us how we should address God in our prayers. So in this section we're going to investigate the question: How do the Psalms address or speak to God? In other words, what titles, terms, and images do the psalmists use when they address God? If we're going to allow the Psalms to teach us how to pray, surely this is where we need to begin. How should we address this God to whom we're praying?

Extra Steps:

When you pray, do you have a favorite way of addressing God? If so, what is it, and why is it meaningful to you? If you don't have a favorite title for God, what are some of the ways you do refer to God when you pray?

Listen carefully to the public prayers in the worship services at your church. Notice the various ways the pastor, priest, or liturgist addresses God. How do those forms of address shape your thinking about God as you pray along with the worship leader?

Why might it be valuable to learn to pray using more variety in our names for God?

---

3. Willard, *Hearing God*, 20.

I'd been a follower of Jesus for quite a few years when I became aware of a habit I'd fallen into in the way I prayed. I was reflecting on my prayer life one day, and I realized that whenever I prayed out loud, I almost always started my prayers with "Lord, . . ." Nothing complicated, just "Lord." Now there's certainly nothing wrong with addressing God as Lord. After all, that's who God is! But as I thought more about it, I became convinced that being so limited in how I addressed God was also limiting how I thought about God while I prayed. Calling God "Lord" emphasized his leadership and sovereignty over my life, but what about his love and mercy? His grace and forgiveness? Lord is hardly a term of intimacy. I wondered if perhaps I was keeping God at a distance when "Lord" was almost the only way I addressed him.

So I intentionally began to open my prayers with other titles for God. One of my new favorites was "Gracious and loving God." That emphasized two wonderful qualities about God. In addition, I began constructing and using other titles as well. As I began addressing God in these other ways, I sensed my prayers taking on a more intimate and relational tone. I wasn't just going to my Lord with my needs and requests. Now I was learning to center my prayers in who God is and in what God's done for me. The way I addressed God made a huge difference.

Perhaps this shouldn't be too surprising, because it's also true in our human relationships. Imagine how conversations might differ if they begin with "George," or with "Mrs. Jones," or with "Dr. Franklin," or with "Mr. President." George might be a good friend, and we could anticipate a lively and frank talk with him. Mrs. Jones might be an elderly neighbor, and our conversation with her would be friendly but limited in topics. A conversation with Dr. Franklin might focus on our health, perhaps with the encouragement to drop a few pounds and get more exercise. And if we had the opportunity to speak to the President, we might be so tongue-tied we wouldn't know what to say! Simply by the way we address someone, we have some sense for the nature of the conversation we're going to have—as well as for our relationship with the person. And that's also true with God. The way we address God says much about our understanding of who God is and the relationship we have with God.

In our culture, names generally function as little more than labels. When you learn that my name is Steve, that doesn't tell you much about me. "Steve" is just a convenient way to refer to me or to get my attention. It doesn't tell you who I *really* am. (I *wish* it told you I was as funny as Stephen Colbert, as wealthy as Steve Ballmer, or as athletic as Stephen Curry!)

One exception to this is with nicknames. Nicknames often reveal at least something about a person. For instance, if I mentioned the name "Michael," you might begin thinking of someone named Michael whom you know, but it doesn't tell you anything about the person I have in mind. However, if I said that Michael's nickname is "Air Jordan," you immediately picture him flying through the air with a basketball in his outstretched hand. Or if I tell you that one of my nicknames in junior high was "Beanpole," you have a pretty good idea of what my physique looked like back then. I was six-foot-one and could disappear just by turning sideways. No one calls me Beanpole anymore.

Extra Steps:

Do you know why your parents gave you your particular name? Were they trying to say something special about you?

If you have children, how did you choose their names? Was there some special meaning in the names you chose?

In biblical times, names functioned more like nicknames do today. They weren't just labels, but instead they were often chosen to reflect some characteristic or experience of the person. Thus, knowing someone's name meant knowing something about them. So, for instance, in Genesis 25:26 Jacob was given his name (which means "he grasps the heel") when he came out of his mother's womb holding onto the foot of his twin brother, Esau, who was born just ahead of him. "Jacob" was also a Hebrew expression for a deceiver, and Jacob certainly demonstrated that aspect of his character throughout his lifetime. Later on, however, Jacob had a profound spiritual experience during which he wrestled with a "man" for an entire night (Gen. 32:22–30). Afterwards, the "man" gave Jacob a new name, Israel, which means "he struggles with God." When we know Jacob/Israel's name, we know something about him. This is often the case with biblical names. It's certainly true with God's names.

Names for God in the Psalms

In the book of Psalms, the two most common names for God are "God" (I suppose that's pretty obvious) and "Lord" (generally written with small capital letters).

"God" is the general word for deity in the Bible, and in the Old Testament it usually translates the Hebrew word *'elohîm*. *'Elohîm* is actually the plural form of *'el*, a word that means strong and mighty, and so this name emphasizes God's power and might. Although it's a generic term—an abstract noun rather than a personal name—the Bible regularly uses it as a personal name, and it's capitalized to indicate that usage ("God"). In some contexts, however, *'elohîm* may be rendered as "gods" (e.g., Ps. 138:1).

Some translators add the honorific "O" when "God" is used in direct address, perhaps to further distinguish the word and make it seem more reverent, even though there's no Hebrew word for the "O." So, for example, at the beginning of Psalm 51 the *NIV* reads, "Have mercy on me, O God." However, the *NIV* is not consistent in this practice and will often omit the "O" even in direct address (e.g., Ps. 60:1). Whether we add the "O" or not, this is the most general (and impersonal) way we can address God.

The other name by which God is most often addressed in the Psalms is "Lord," which translates the Hebrew word *Yahweh*. Whereas "God" is a nonpersonal name, *Yahweh* is the covenant name for God, the name God told Moses to call him. When God appeared to Moses at the burning bush, Moses said he would need some way to refer to God when he spoke to the Israelites. So God told him to say to the people, "*Yahweh* . . . has sent me to you" (Exod. 3:13–15). The name *Yahweh* is related to the verb *hayah*, which means "to be," but the precise meaning of *Yahweh* has engendered considerable debate among scholars. However, there's no disagreement that it's intended as a personal name, recalling God's covenantal relationship with his people.

The spelling of *Yahweh* has also generated some confusion. *Yahweh* actually consists of four Hebrew consonants, *YHWH*, with no vowels, because vowels were not used in the original Hebrew text. Although linguistic scholars are in general agreement about which vowels should be added (which is how we end up with *Yahweh*), the Jews considered the name *Yahweh* to be so holy that it was never pronounced, lest the speaker accidentally misuse God's name (see Exod. 20:7). So whenever they were reading and came upon the name *YHWH* in the Hebrew text, they would pronounce the ordinary word for "Lord" (*'Adonai*) instead. Today, *Hashem*, meaning "The Name," is sometimes substituted instead.

A WALKING CONVERSATION

Although non-Jews generally have no reservations about speaking the name *Yahweh*, our modern translations have generally acceded to the Jewish practice by substituting "Lord" (with small capital letters) wherever the Hebrew text has *Yahweh*.

When vowels were eventually added to the Hebrew text, the vowels for *'Adonai* ("Lord") were added to the consonants YHWH. In 1611 the *King James Version* transliterated that hybrid name into "Jehovah" (Y and J are often used for the same Hebrew letter). Due to the popularity of the *KJV*, "Jehovah" entered the lexicon of names for God even though it isn't an accurate translation of the Hebrew text.

Translating *Yahweh* with the word "Lord" is a bit unfortunate, however, because one is a personal name and the other is a non-personal title. The title "Lord" emphasizes sovereignty and authority, both of which certainly apply to God, but it lacks the relational dimension of the covenant name *Yahweh*. Another negative is that "Lord" is a masculine term ("Lady" being the feminine opposite), while *Yahweh* has no gender implied. Bernhard Anderson points out that this isn't as much of a problem in English, because "Lord" is rather archaic and for that reason is not immediately associated with males. However, he notes that *Yahweh* is rendered in German as "der Herr" and in Spanish as "El Señor." Each of those is the normal way to address a male in those languages.[4] In spite of these drawbacks, however, nearly every modern translation of the Bible uses "Lord" to represent this personal name for God. One exception is the *New Jerusalem Bible*, which simply uses "Yahweh."

Evidently, the psalmists themselves had their own personal preferences for how to address God. Compare Psalms 14 and 53, and you'll see that they're nearly identical, except that Psalm 14 uses *Yahweh* ("Lord"), while Psalm 53 uses *'Elohîm* ("God"). In general, the Psalms overwhelmingly prefer to use "Lord." However, the section from Psalm 42–83 uses "God" about five times more often than "Lord," and for that reason it's sometimes called the "Elohistic Psalter" because of this dominant way of addressing God.

This may seem a bit confusing, perhaps, but as we read and pray the Psalms, it's important that we not miss the personal nature of this name for God. God is our Lord, yes, but God's so much more than that! He's also the God who has invited us to call him by his personal name, *Yahweh*. He's the God who has chosen to enter into a covenantal relationship with his people

---

4. Anderson, *Out of the Depths*, 14–15.

and be on a first-name basis with them. Please remember that whenever you see "Lord" used for God's name.

The third-most-common name for God in the Old Testament is *'Adonai*, which is the ordinary Hebrew word for "Lord" or "Master." This name/title occurs only a fraction as often as *Yahweh* or *'Elohîm*, and when it does, it's generally printed without the small caps in order to distinguish it from *Yahweh* (i.e., "Lord" instead of "Lord"). The name *'Adonai* carries with it the idea of ownership. God is our *'Adonai*, or Lord, because God created us and therefore owns us. God is our Master, our *'Adonai*, and we are God's servants.

All three of these names (*'Elohîm, Yahweh,* and *'Adonai*) also appear in a multitude of variations and combinations. Some of the ones you'll encounter in the Psalms include "God Almighty," "Sovereign Lord," "Lord Most High," "Lord of Hosts" (often translated as "Lord Almighty"), "my God," and so forth.

In addition to these names and titles for God, the psalmists use numerous metaphors to address or refer to God. "King," "Rock," and "Shepherd" are used frequently, but there are many, many others. In his book on using the Psalms in worship, John Witvliet provides "a sampling of names for God in the Psalms," a "sampling" that includes fifty-seven different ones![5]

Extra Steps:

Scan through at least ten psalms and find as many different names, titles, or metaphors for God as you can. For example, in Psalm 19:14 God is referred to as Lord, *Rock, and Redeemer. As we've discussed, "*Lord*" is the covenant name for God. "Rock" is a metaphor, comparing God to the strength and permanence of a rock. And "Redeemer" is a title, one that refers to God's role as the one who delivers his people. What other names, titles, and metaphors for God can you find?*

Are All of the Psalms Prayers?

As you read around in the Psalms, you'll quickly notice that they don't always speak directly to God. Often a psalm is addressed to God, as we might expect a prayer to be, but not always. Many psalms speak *about* God, using the third-person. When God himself isn't being addressed, the psalm may

---

5. Witvliet, *Psalms in Christian Worship*, 18–20.

be addressed to the people of Israel (e.g., Ps. 67:1: "May God be gracious to us and bless us and make his face shine on us"), or the nations (Ps. 47:1: "Clap your hands, all you nations"), or even the entire earth (Ps. 100:1: "Shout for joy to the LORD, all the earth"). On occasion, the psalm may be framed as though the psalmist were speaking to himself, as in Psalms 103 and 104, which both begin with the exhortation, "Praise the LORD, my soul."

Even within individual Psalms, however, the audience sometimes shifts. Consider the opening of Psalm 104:

> ¹ Praise the LORD, my soul.
> ² LORD my God, you are very great;
>   you are clothed with splendor and majesty.
> ³ The LORD wraps himself in light as with a garment;
>   he stretches out the heavens like a tent
>   and lays the beams of his upper chambers on their waters.

The psalmist begins with a self-address ("my soul"), but in verse 2 he switches and speaks directly to God. Then in verse 3 he talks about God in the third-person, as though he's speaking to his soul or to some other audience. These shifts occur throughout the psalm: sometimes the psalm talks *to* God, sometimes it talks *about* God.

Psalm 67 is another good example of this shifting of audience. The psalm begins by addressing the people, but then it immediately breaks off and speaks directly to God:

> ¹ May God be gracious to us and bless us
>   and make his face shine on us—
> ² so that your ways may be known on earth,
>   your salvation among all nations.

Verses 3–5 continue to speak to God, but then the psalm closes by speaking to the people and talking about God in the third-person once again in verses 6–7. The psalm concludes with a benediction similar to the opening verse: "May God bless us still, so that all the ends of the earth will fear him."

What are we to make of these observations? We normally expect prayers to be addressed to God. Does this mean that those psalms which have a different audience are not actually prayers, but something else? Something more like a testimony perhaps, or even a short sermon? And what do we make out of those psalms where the psalmist switches his audience, like Psalms 104 and 67 above? Are those psalms only partial prayers?

Perhaps the problem lies in our limited view of prayer. I've come to see the shifting between addressing God directly and speaking to oneself or to a third party as evidence of the conversational nature of prayer. As Walter Brueggemann writes, "I am struck in powerful ways by how the praying voices in the Psalter are passionately *dialogical*."[6] He goes on to say how he believes the Psalms are "deeply interactive" and are "a genuinely two-party enterprise."

As I've worked with the Psalms, I've come to greatly appreciate this dialogical and interactive aspect. Some psalms give voice to my words to God. Other times God is speaking to me through the psalmist's words. Even when a psalm makes it seem as though I'm speaking to myself, it's like these words are my inner thoughts about God. When we converse with another person, we often do the same thing. We speak words to the person, but we also have thoughts about the person that we don't verbalize out loud. For example, when Carol and I are going out someplace, I might tell her how beautiful she looks, but at the same time I might also say to myself, "How blessed I am to have her for my wife!" That outward and inward dialogue is an integral part of conversation. And when we pray the Psalms, that outward and inward dialogue is also going on. However, that doesn't make any of the psalms less prayerful, because God hears our inner thoughts just as much as he hears our spoken words. *Thus, all of the psalms become prayers whenever we speak them in the presence of God.* When we do that, every one of the 150 psalms becomes a prayer to God—whether the words are addressed directly to God or spoken about God.

Extra Steps:

What do you think of the idea that words can be part of a prayer even if they aren't directly addressed to God? If you don't accept that understanding of prayer, then how do you view those psalms (and parts of psalms) that are not addressed to God? If they aren't prayers, then what are they?

Hearing God Through the Psalms

But now I want to turn to the other side of the conversation. When God chooses to speak to us, how does he do that? What should we expect to

---

6. Brueggemann, *Praying the Psalms*, xiv (emphasis his).

hear? To help us think about this, let me tell you about an experience I had not too long ago.

Early one Sunday morning, the light of dawn was just beginning to turn back the darkness as Emma and I were heading out for another walk. Usually, I'll bring flashcards of particular psalms to recite and pray through as we walk. But not this morning. The previous day had been a rather lousy one for me. I had been angry and upset over several things, and I was feeling down and discouraged. I certainly wasn't feeling very spiritual this morning. In fact, I wasn't even sure I wanted to talk with God on this walk. That's never a good feeling, but my guilt was amplified by the fact that in a few hours I was scheduled to be the guest preacher at a small church in Idaho. Kind of hard to speak *for* God when you don't really want to speak *to* God. But that's the way I felt.

We had barely left the driveway, however, when the opening line of Psalm 51 popped into my thoughts: "Have mercy on me, O God, according to your unfailing love." Immediately, I knew I needed to pray that psalm. So as we walked towards the nature preserve near our home, I prayed those words that David had prayed when he realized he needed God's forgiveness and reconciliation. My mood began to change a bit.

When I finished Psalm 51, I began to pray Psalm 86. I had recently memorized that psalm, and I try to pray those new psalms at least once a day for several weeks. Psalm 86 begins, "Hear me, Lord, and answer me, for I am poor and needy." That certainly described the way I was feeling. So I continued to pray my way through that psalm as Emma and I meandered along the trail in the nature preserve.

Near the end of the psalm I came to the psalmist's final request of God: "Give me a sign of your goodness." As I spoke those words, I glanced up, and a deer pranced through the meadow, no more than fifty feet in front of us. The deer paused for a few moments on the path ahead of us, looked right at us—as if to say, "Good morning!"—and then ran off towards the safety of the nearby woods.

As you've probably gathered from reading this book, I love animals. And I always consider it a special treat to see a deer. They're such beautiful creatures! But the timing of this morning's deer sighting convinced me that this was intended for me as "a sign of [God's] goodness." I had confessed my sin, and this was God's way of assuring me I was forgiven. God was giving me a sign of his goodness, mercy, and grace. At that moment, I felt a surge of joy and gratitude. My earlier funk was gone. As Emma and I began to make our way back home, the dawn was painting the few scattered clouds with hues of red and yellow. I found myself praying the words of Psalm 8, "You have set your glory in the heavens...."

God spoke to me that morning—at least twice. First, I believe God spoke to me by bringing the words of Psalm 51:1 into my thoughts. Then, as I was praying Psalm 86, God used the deer to say to me, "Steve, I'm going to show you how good I am. I'm going to show you that I love you and that all that stuff yesterday is past history, forgiven and wiped from my memory banks." In all this, I didn't hear any audible words, but I heard God nonetheless. I was reminded again that holy walks are not just times for us to speak to God, but they're also times when we listen for God to speak to us. Holy walks are indeed walking conversations.

As you reflect on my experience that morning, you may wonder how I can be so sure that God was speaking to me. Actually, I believe God speaks to each of us far more often than we ever realize. We don't hear him, however, because God speaks in ways that are different from what we expect or because we haven't learned to recognize the "sound" of God's voice. So the real question we need to answer is, *When we're praying the Psalms (and at other times as well), how can we hear God's voice?* To answer that, we first need to understand the nature of God's voice and how God usually speaks to his people.

Understanding the Nature of God's Voice

If God were to speak to you, what would you expect his voice to sound like? Charlton Heston? Morgan Freeman? Della Reese? Someone else? Take a moment and reflect on what you might expect to hear.

Extra Steps:

Have you had an experience where you believe God was speaking directly to you? Reflect on that experience. How did you know it was God who was speaking? What did God tell you? How did you respond? How did that experience impact your life?

If you have not had an experience where you believe God spoke to you, why do you suppose that is?

People sometimes expect that if God were to speak to them, it would be in some powerful and dramatic fashion, like a burning bush or at least a booming baritone. However, we should remember that there's only one burning bush recorded in the Bible. If we're expecting to hear a heavenly loudspeaker blaring forth the divine Voice, we'll probably be left waiting for a very long time.

Instead, we ought to take note of how God spoke to the prophet Elijah in 1 Kings 19. Outside a cave on Mt. Horeb, Elijah didn't hear God's voice in a mighty wind, or an earthquake, or a fire, but rather in "a gentle whisper" (v. 12). God's lesson was clear: when God speaks, he doesn't need to shout or overpower us. Usually, God speaks to us quietly, like someone gently whispering to us.

In fact, we may not even hear an audible sound at all (I never have). Instead, God's voice may come to us *in our mind*, like a fleeting thought. In his book, *God Is Closer Than You Think*, John Ortberg says that, because God is infinite, "he is able to guide our thoughts directly. He can speak to us through Scripture, of course, or through the words of another person. But he also has 'direct access,' so to speak; he can plant a thought directly in our minds. Anytime. Anywhere."[7] Indeed, that may be the most common way God speaks to us: in the very words that make up our own thoughts.

So, rather than expecting God's voice to be some kind of booming, heavenly declaration, we need to learn to listen for those gentle whispers. We may "hear" those gentle whispers as a quiet, inner voice, but perhaps most often, they'll come to us as thoughts, thoughts that cause us to wonder: *Where did* that *come from?* Or, *Why hadn't I considered* that *before?* Or, *Why was I suddenly thinking about* that *person?*

Think back to the Sunday morning incident I described earlier. Was Psalm 51 simply a random thought? Was the deer sighting just a coincidence? Some people—perhaps *most* people—might think so. But I'm not sure there's ever such a thing as "random thoughts" or "coincidences" when we're on a holy walk. I wouldn't be surprised to learn that God had sent one of his angels (heavenly messengers) to tell that deer to go stand by the path right at the precise moment I'd be coming by. When we know we're walking in the presence of God, the things around us (deer, sunrises, gentle breezes, etc.) take on new meaning, and even our thoughts become charged in special ways.

---

7. Ortberg, *God Is Closer*, 86.

We often speak of being in a *personal* relationship with God, but God actually wants much more than that. When we fail to hear God's gentle whispers, Dallas Willard says it's because we haven't grasped God's desire for us to be in a *conversational* relationship with him, not just a personal one.[8] God speaks to us in order to nurture that kind of relationship. God isn't interested in just passing along bits of information to us. Rather, by speaking to us, God wants to shape our heart and character to be like his, so that we can be God's holy conversation partners.

Jesus himself made that clear in the way he described his relationship with his followers. He said, "I am the good shepherd; I know my sheep and my sheep know me—just as my Father knows me and I know my Father" (John 10:14–15). In other words, Jesus envisions the same kind of relationship with his followers as he has with his heavenly Father. Wow! But then it gets even more amazing. He added, "My sheep listen to my voice; I know them and they follow me" (John 10:27). Let that settle into your mind. Jesus speaks to his followers, and those people who are truly following him hear his voice and respond to it, just like sheep hear and respond to the voice of their shepherd.

But Jesus' followers aren't just sheep. Later, Jesus said, "I have called you friends, for everything that I learned from my Father I have made known to you" (John 15:15). Thus, Jesus views his followers as friends who both listen and speak with him. Evidently, he wants to have a relationship with each of us like the one God had with Moses: "The LORD would speak to Moses face to face, as one speaks to a friend" (Exod. 33:11). That's the kind of relationship Jesus is saying that he wants with each one of us: a conversational relationship, like two good friends might have with each other.

Now I don't want to skip by this too quickly. It's truly amazing that the eternal God, the God who created and sustains everything that exists, likes to speak to creatures that he created: people like you and me. But it's true, and the Bible is filled with stories of God speaking to all kinds of men and women. This means that God wants to speak to you just as much as he invites you to speak to him. Do you really believe that? Do you believe that God wants to have a conversational relationship with *you*?

If that seems hard to believe, you might reflect on the relationship I have with my dog Emma. Obviously, you know by now that I do a lot of walking with her. But in addition to walking, I also do a lot of talking to her—and I really like doing that. And, amazingly enough, sometimes she

---

8. Willard, *Hearing God*, 35.

even listens to me. She often seems to know exactly what I'm saying to her, especially if my sentences include words like "dinner" or "treat." On those occasions, she responds to my voice by jumping up and down, wagging her stubby little tail, and just generally getting all excited. Of course, most of the time when we're out walking, she could care less about anything I might say. When we're outside, she's easily distracted by all the wonderful smells and, of course, by all the evil squirrels that she's convinced are taking over the world. But, even then, I still talk to her, simply because I like to.

Now, does it seem strange to you that I talk to my dog? Perhaps it does for non-pet-owners, but if you have a dog (or any other kind of pet), I can almost guarantee that you speak to him or her. It's just what we dog-owners do. We love to talk to our dogs. In a similar way, God loves to speak to his people, people like you and me. So, when I find myself speaking to Emma, I remind myself that God also delights in speaking to me. Now, if only I could learn to listen to God's voice better than Emma listens to mine!

Learning To Recognize God's Voice

So we need to understand that God delights in speaking to us but that God usually does so in a quiet voice, often in the very thoughts that run through our mind. That leads, however, to the question, "How do I know when it's truly *God* speaking?" After all, we live in a noisy world, with all kinds of voices clamoring for our attention, and our minds are filled with jumbles of thoughts. How do we recognize God's quiet voice in the midst of all that? The simple answer is that we *learn* to do that. It takes experience.

In the early years of my marriage, my mother-in-law would often call to chat with Carol and me (mostly with Carol). This was back in the days before Caller ID, and so every time the phone rang you wondered who was calling. Most callers would introduce themselves as soon as you picked up the phone. However, my mother-in-law would simply say, "Hi!" That was it. Just the one word. Then silence, as she waited for me to say something. The first several times this happened I found myself wracking my brain for who the caller might be. It wasn't too long, however, before I learned to recognize my mother-in-law's voice in just that single word "Hi." In a similar way, it takes some experience for us to learn to recognize God's voice when he chooses to speak to us.

In his book, *Hearing God*, Dallas Willard points out several factors that distinguish God's voice.[9] Just as human voices have certain qualities that enable us to tell one person's voice from someone else's (accents, tone, spirit, and so forth), Willard notes that God's voice also has unique qualities:

- One is that God's voice carries a *certain weight or power* and just impresses itself on us. In Mark 1:27 we're told that Jesus taught "as one who had authority." His words had a certain power and authority. And that's always true of God's voice.

- Another quality is that God's voice brings a *sense of peace and confidence and joy*. It certainly isn't that God's voice promises to relieve all suffering or challenge—far from it! But even in the midst of a difficult situation, God's voice always brings grace and peace.

- A third quality of God's voice is that it will always be *consistent with God's written Word*, with the Scriptures. God will never speak a word to us that contradicts the words God has already spoken to us in the Bible.

Those are some of the distinguishing qualities of God's voice, but it still takes experience to learn to recognize when God is speaking to us. We don't always recognize God's voice immediately—just like the boy Samuel didn't when God first spoke to him (1 Sam. 3). When we first begin following Jesus, we often do so with only a vague sense of God's presence from time to time. As we grow in our faith, we become more aware of God's acts, of things that God has done on our behalf, or ways that God has blessed us or touched our lives. Part of becoming mature followers of Jesus is that we learn to recognize the voice of our Shepherd. We learn to listen for and hear God's voice speaking to us.

But how do we get that experience in learning to listen for God's voice? This is where a spiritual practice like holy walks is so beneficial. When we set out on a holy walk, we're telling God that we want to listen to him. We're inviting God to speak to us, if he so chooses, and we're intentionally opening our spiritual ears to listen for God's gentle whispers. In her book *The Power of Listening*, Lynne Baab explains why we need to do this:

> To think that we will hear God's voice easily and frequently without making space for God in our lives is one of the myths of our time. The Holy Spirit works in amazing and surprising ways, to be sure, and God's voice does indeed break into our lives in unexpected

---

9. Willard, *Hearing God*, 227.

ways. Yet God's voice is often still and small, and we usually need to slow down in order to hear it.... Spiritual practices make space for hearing God's voice of love and guidance, because they show our desire to listen.[10]

When we want to have a serious conversation with a friend, we probably won't do it in the middle of a busy train station. Instead, we'll look for a quiet coffee shop, or a bench in a park, or a peaceful walking path—someplace where we can both speak and listen comfortably. That's a way of showing how much we value the friendship and desire to hear what our friend wants to say. Holy walks work in a similar way, only now our conversation partner is God himself.

There are no formulas or methods for manipulating God into speaking whenever or however we wish him to. God speaks when *he* chooses to speak. But as we make the effort to listen for God's voice, I believe we'll begin to hear God speaking to us more and more. We'll hear God's voice not just when we need special direction or help, but throughout our days. We'll hear God's voice leading us. We'll hear God's words of grace and peace and assurance. And we'll find ourselves living life in a conversational relationship with the God who created us, who redeemed us, and who promised to be with us always. May it always be so.

Extra Steps:

Reflect on a conversation that you had with a good friend. Where did it take place? Who initiated it? What made it special?

In what ways do you think a conversation with God is similar to, and different from, the conversation you had with your friend?

---

10. Baab, *Power of Listening*, 103–4.

Chapter 5

Exercising the Heart

"Whom have I in heaven but you?
And earth has nothing I desire besides you.
My flesh and my heart may fail,
but God is the strength of my heart
and my portion forever."

—Psalm 73:25–26

ONE SIDE-BENEFIT OF WALKING the dog while I pray the Psalms is that I get some physical exercise every day. (I once read that instead of making a New Year's resolution to walk every day, you should just get a dog. Then you'll walk every day for a decade.) Walking is good for me physiologically, because it pumps some extra oxygen through my cardiovascular system and provides me with an aerobic workout. That's the kind of exercise benefit we usually think of when it comes to walking—and I do appreciate that aspect. However, far more important to me is the spiritual benefit. Holy walks are good exercises for me because they also pump God's Word into my heart. As I walk and pray the Psalms, God's Word circulates in my heart and mind, even as my blood circulates in my arteries and veins. Quite simply, walking and praying the Psalms is a great spiritual workout for the heart.

Now I don't have to be an expert on exercise physiology to benefit from working out, but it probably helps to understand some of the basic principles. In a similar way, when we decide to exercise our heart by praying the Psalms, it helps to understand some basics. We don't have to be biblical scholars to derive great benefit from praying the Psalms, but it does help to have at least some understanding of the background and nature of the Psalms.

So in this chapter I want to give you a short introduction to the book of Psalms. Perhaps you already know most of this and want to just skim through this material. Feel free to do that. But you may find a refresher to be helpful, and some of this may be new to you as well. My goal is to provide you with just enough information about the Psalms that you can start your own practice of heart-learning and prayer-walking with the Psalms. Later, as you spend more time with the Psalms, you may be motivated to do some in-depth study of the Psalms on your own. At the end of this book, I've provided a bibliography which lists some resources that can help you do that if you so desire.

Extra Steps:

From what you presently know about the Psalms, how would you describe them to someone who has no familiarity with the Bible?

After you finish reading this chapter, reflect on how you might answer that question differently.

Getting Acquainted with the Psalms

Before reading this introduction to the Psalms, put this book down and take a few minutes to glance through the book of Psalms. (Psalms is an easy book to locate in the Bible: just let your Bible fall open in the middle and you're probably there—or at least very close.) For this exercise, try to view the book of Psalms as though you've never read it before. So take at least five or ten minutes to skim through the book with fresh eyes and see what you notice. If you have access to different translations of the Bible and want to invest a little more time in this exercise, compare those versions and look for editorial and layout differences. Go ahead and get started. I'll still be here when you're finished.

* * *

All right, what did you see? The rest of this section explains and amplifies some of the things you may have noticed. You probably saw many other things as well—we never exhaust our ability to learn more about God's

Word. However, these are some of the basic characteristics and facts about the Psalms that you will want to be aware of.

First, the *title* of the book. You didn't skip over that, did you? In the *New International Version*, the title of the collection is simply "Psalms." Other translations entitle it "The Psalms" or "The Book of Psalms." Have you ever wondered where that title comes from?

The Hebrew name for the book is *Tehillîm,* which comes from the same root as the more familiar Hebrew word *Hallelûjah* and means "Praises" or "Songs of Praise." In the second or third century, BC, the Hebrew scriptures were translated into Greek, a translation commonly known as the Septuagint.[1] In the Septuagint, the book of *Tehillîm* was given the title *Psalmoi*, which is the plural of the Greek word *psalmos* ("song"). Then, in the late-fourth century, the pope commissioned a biblical scholar by the name of Jerome to translate the Bible into Latin. Jerome's translation, called the Vulgate,[2] simply transliterated the title *Psalmoi* into Latin, and that was how it entered into our English translations much later on. Frequently, the book of Psalms is also referred to as "The Psalter," which comes from the Greek word *psalterion*, meaning a collection of *psalmoi* or songs.

But what exactly is a *"psalm"*? Here's my definition: "A psalm is a sacred song or poem used as a prayer to God." Notice that this definition expresses both the *form* and the *purpose* of a psalm. Not every prayer is a psalm, just as not every song or poem is a prayer. But when we compose a song or poem as a prayer to God, then we've written a psalm. That's what the authors of the biblical psalms did. They wrote songs/poems as prayers to the God they loved and served.

This means it's important to keep in mind that the biblical psalms are not essays, epistles, sermons, or theological treatises. Each of the 150 psalms originated in a heart of faith—although at times a faith that was

---

1. The Septuagint (commonly abbreviated as LXX) represented the first time the Hebrew scriptures were translated into another language. The translation took place during the time of the Greek Empire, when most Jews spoke Greek as their primary language. Tradition holds that seventy-two scholars miraculously translated the entire Old Testament in just seventy-two days. The Septuagint served as the "Bible" for Greek-speaking Jews in many countries prior to and after the coming of Jesus Christ. It's often the version which is quoted in the New Testament.

2. The word "Vulgate" means "common" or "popular," and it became the primary version of the Bible used by the church until the fifteenth century, when numerous other translations began to appear as part of the Protestant Reformation. In 1546 the Council of Trent declared the Vulgate to be the only authentic Latin translation, and it remains the official Bible of the Roman Catholic Church to this day.

severely challenged—and each psalm expresses that faith to God, thus making them a form of prayer. Many of them are very personal in nature; others are more befitting a corporate prayer. Yet, all of them are prayers, even those which aren't addressed directly to God or which don't seem to take a prayer format. I'll explore the purposes of various psalms in chapters 6, 7, and 8.

If you skimmed all the way to the end of the book of Psalms, you also noticed (or already knew) that there's a total of *150 psalms* in the collection.[3] A less obvious observation that you also may have noticed is that the Psalms are divided into *five "books."* Book I is made up of Psalms 1–41, Book II consists of Psalms 42–72, Book III includes Psalms 73–89, Book IV contains Psalms 90–106, and Book V completes the fivefold division with Psalms 107–150. Each of the first four books concludes with a one- or two-verse declaration of praise which serves as a doxology for the book, and the entirety of Psalm 150 serves as a doxology for Book V as well as for the entire book of Psalms.

It isn't known when this division occurred, but it's quite ancient, at least two thousand years old. The reason for it also is elusive. There's little in the content of the Psalms that would explain the division. Most likely it was related to the process of gathering the Psalms into the collection we have today. The book of Psalms obviously was not written by a single author at a single time, such as Luke writing his Gospel account, or the Apostle Paul penning one of his letters. Instead, the Psalms are the literary product of numerous authors, who wrote at various times. As time went by, some of those psalms were gathered into smaller collections, such as ones attributed to Korah (Pss. 42–49) or to Asaph (Pss. 73–83) and the Psalms of Ascent (Pss. 120–134), which we discussed in chapter 2. The whole process took more than five hundred years, but eventually those smaller collections were gathered with other psalms, and the book of Psalms as we know it took shape. We can see that some of these smaller collections helped to shape the fivefold division of the Psalter.

However, another purpose was likely at work as well in this division. By dividing the Psalms into five books, a parallel was created with the five books of the *Torah*, or the Law.[4] According to this theory, early editors

---

3. Actually, the Septuagint contains a 151st psalm but acknowledges that it is "outside the number" (i.e., it is not part of the traditional 150).

4. Genesis, Exodus, Leviticus, Numbers, and Deuteronomy. These first five books of the Bible are also sometimes called the Pentateuch, a Greek word that means "five-volumed." These five books have been grouped together since ancient times. The *Torah/*

thought that the *Tehillîm*, as the Book of David (to whom nearly half of the psalms are attributed), should have five parts just as the *Torah*, the Book of Moses, has five parts. So they divided the collection on that basis. That's an intriguing and plausible idea, but, whatever the original reason for this fivefold division of the Psalms, it serves little practical purpose in our study or use of the Psalms.

Perhaps you also noticed that the text is printed in *poetic format*. Portions of many other biblical books are printed in a similar format, but most of the Bible is printed in standard paragraph formatting like we're accustomed to in non-biblical books. This poetic formatting occurs in nearly every translation of the Bible, with one significant exception: the *King James Version*. If you normally use the *KJV*, you likely missed the poetic nature of the book of Psalms. This is because the translators of the *KJV* decided to make each verse into a standalone unit. This is true for every book in the *KJV* Bible: the *Torah*, the Prophets, the Gospels, the Epistles—everything, including the Psalms.

I believe this was a huge mistake on the part of these translators. Having verse divisions as the organizing factor in the translation obscures the literary nature of the biblical books. The *KJV* formatting presents each book of the Bible as a collection of individual verses instead of as a literary whole. However, people speak and write in paragraphs, not in verses. In addition, the verse divisions and numbering were never part of the original writing; they were added much later and often not in the best places to convey the writer's thoughts. Perhaps one unfortunate legacy of the *KJV*'s decision is the way many people pick and choose favorite verses instead of studying and appreciating each biblical book as a whole. This is especially true with the Psalms, where we often select individual verses that sound good to us, but we ignore the meaning of the verse within the context of the entire psalm. Fortunately, most other translations format the Psalms as poetry.

If you noticed the poetical format, you may also have realized that it isn't the kind of poetry we're accustomed to reading. For one thing, the lines don't rhyme. Nor is there any apparent meter or rhythm. If you picked up on those differences, give yourself a pat on the back, because that's extremely significant. Hebrew poetry is built on "*thought* rhymes," not on rhyming *sounds*, as we generally think of in traditional poetry. The

---

Law/Pentateuch is one of the three major divisions in the Hebrew scriptures. The other two divisions are the Prophets and the Writings. The book of Psalms is the first book in the Writings section.

difference is quite important, and grasping this aspect of Hebrew poetry is critical for understanding and praying the Psalms. I'll talk more about this in the next section.

Something else you likely observed is that most of the psalms have some kind of *title or superscription*. In fact, that's true for more than three-fourths of them (116 in total). Look, for example, at Psalm 3. Between the heading "Psalm 3" and the start of verse 1, we read: "A psalm of David. When he fled from his son Absalom." This superscription seems to provide the name of the author (David), as well as the circumstances under which this particular psalm was written (see 2 Sam. 15:14). If you don't find this or other superscriptions in your Bible, that's because a few modern translations have chosen to omit them (e.g., *The New English Bible*) or to move them to the footnotes at the bottom of the pages (e.g., *Today's English Version*, also known as *The Good News Bible*). You may be using one of those versions, in which case you might want to check out a different translation to see this feature of the Psalms.

Most of these superscriptions were probably not a part of the psalms when they were originally written, but it's possible that a few were. For example, in Psalm 18 the heading seems to lead right into the first verse of the psalm, indicating that it may have been part of the psalm when it was first composed. All of these superscriptions appeared very early, however, and are included in the Septuagint, which places them at least as far back as the second century, BC.

In addition to authorship and historical context like we see in Psalm 3, many of the superscriptions contain various musical and liturgical instructions (see, e.g., Pss. 4, 5, and 6), and some also identify the type of psalm. The most common of those types is the *mizmôr*, a Hebrew word that means "song" or "instrumental music" but which is usually translated as "psalm," as it is in the superscription for Psalm 3. In addition, many superscriptions contain technical terms where the meaning is uncertain. In those cases the Hebrew word is generally transliterated into English and a footnote provided. You can find information on those terms in commentaries or a good Bible dictionary, if you wish to know more.

The *musical nature* of many of these superscriptions indicates that the Psalms were something more than just a collection of prayers. Many, if not all, of them were also written to be part of Israel's hymnody. Put to music, the Psalms were an important tool for worship by the ancient Israelites. Much later, Christians frequently sang or chanted the Psalms in their own worship services. Some Christians even argued that the Psalms are the *only* proper source for their worship songs. Although I'm not convinced we should go to that extreme, this musical dimension justifies a label numerous writers have ascribed to the Psalms: *The Hymnbook of God's People*.

As someone who's musically-challenged, I have largely ignored the musical aspect of the Psalms in my own work. However, music, like poetry, has a special way of touching the heart and the soul, so bringing music and the Psalms together is natural, if not inevitable. As John Witvliet has observed, "The Psalms cry out to be sung."[5] Because of that, many people find singing to be a meaningful way to pray the Psalms, as well as an aid for learning them. One of those is a close friend of mine who has a deep appreciation for both music and the Psalms. She plays the piano and wrote to tell me how much she enjoys playing hymns that are paraphrases of the Psalms. She also loves listening to the Australian band, The Sons of Korah, who sing the Psalms without many changes in the wording.

Although music can bring the Psalms alive for many people, Witvliet points out that many of the metrical versions of the Psalms are adaptations of the biblical text. Thus, the words in those songs can vary widely from the biblical text, which means that people are rarely singing the actual psalm itself.[6] For that reason, I prefer to stick to the various biblical translations for my own memory work. Well, that and the fact that I can't carry a tune!

Although I haven't incorporated music in my own use of the Psalms, you may find that to be a helpful way to engage the Psalms. If you wish to explore further the musical use of the Psalms, I recommend you check out Witvliet's book, *The Biblical Psalms in Christian Worship: A Brief Introduction and Guide to Resources*.

Returning once again to those superscriptions, you probably noticed that *David* is far and away the individual named most frequently in them. This, of course, refers to King David, the shepherd boy who became Israel's most famous king, reigning from approximately 1000 to 960 BC. Seventy-two of the psalms are attributed to him, and thirteen are said to refer to specific events in his life, such as in Psalm 3. Psalms 34, 51, and 52 are additional examples of that.

Biblical scholars debate how many of these psalms were actually written by David. That's because the Hebrew preposition, *l^e*, which is often translated as "of" in these superscriptions, can have many meanings. So the phrase "of

---

5. Witvliet, *Psalms in Christian Worship*, 94.
6. Witvliet, *Psalms in Christian Worship*, 111.

David" (as in the superscription of Psalm 3) can mean "by David," indicating authorship, but it can also mean "to David" or "for David," indicating some sort of dedication. Or it could even mean something like "about David." We can see this variation of meaning by comparing Psalms 21 and 23, both of which have the superscription "A psalm of David." However, Psalm 21 talks about the king (presumably David) in the third-person and uses "we" in the closing verse, while Psalm 23 speaks entirely in the first-person. It seems reasonable to conclude that Psalm 23 was written by David himself as a personal expression of his faith in God, but Psalm 21 was written to honor David and to be used by the people in a corporate setting.

Because of this ambiguity, scholars aren't certain that David actually wrote each of the seventy-two psalms attributed to him. However, in spite of that uncertainty, we do know that his contribution to the Psalms was enormous. While we can't be certain that David was the author of any particular psalm, that most surely doesn't diminish his importance in the tradition that developed the book of Psalms.

Other authors besides David who are specifically identified in the superscriptions include the Sons of Korah (Pss. 42, 44–49, 84–85, and 87–88), Asaph (Pss. 50 and 73–83), Solomon (Pss. 72 and 127), Ethan the Ezrahite (Ps. 89), and Moses (Ps. 90). The Sons of Korah refers to a guild of temple musicians. Asaph was a Levite appointed by David as a leader of choral music (1 Chr. 16:4–5). Solomon, of course, was David's son and succeeded him as the king of Israel. Ethan the Ezrahite was a wise man who lived during the time of Solomon (1 Kgs. 4:31). And Moses was the one who led the Hebrews out of their bondage in Egypt, through the wilderness, and to the Promised Land. The same uncertainty about David's authorship of particular psalms applies to each of these individuals or groups in regard to the psalms attributed to them.

In this book I frequently refer to the "authors" of various psalms based on these superscriptions. I've chosen to do this for the sake of convenience, even though I fully realize that this may or may not always be accurate. Please keep this in mind.

Speaking about the authorship of the Psalms, we should also note that no woman is mentioned as an author in any of the superscriptions. We can reasonably conclude from this that the vast majority of the psalms were written by men. Nevertheless, in his book, *After Lament*, Glenn Pemberton makes a convincing case that Psalm 131 was likely written by a woman.[7] Although that psalm has the common "Of David" phrase in its superscription, the last part of verse 2 indicates that this is probably the prayer of a nursing mother, rather than David himself: "my soul is like the weaned child that is with me" (*NRSV*). In addition to Psalm 131, since many psalms are anonymous, it's certainly possible that some of those may also have been written by women.

One final observation. As you skimmed through the Psalms, you may also have noticed the word *"Selah"* in the margins of a number of psalms. For instance, in Psalm 3 *Selah* occurs after verses 2, 4, and 8. Although it appears in thirty-nine psalms, *Selah* (pronounced SEE-luh) is a Hebrew word whose precise meaning is unknown. This is why most biblical versions don't even attempt to translate *Selah* but simply transliterate it and relegate it to the margin of the text. In fact, the editors of the 2011 revision of the *NIV* decided not to include this word at all in the body of the psalm. Instead, it is now placed in the footnotes at the bottom of the page each time it occurs. This seems like a reasonable decision, given the uncertainty of the word's meaning or purpose.

Although scholars disagree about the precise meaning of *Selah*, they generally believe it is most likely some sort of musical or worship instruction. Donald Griggs lists three possible interpretations for this instruction.[8] First, he says it could simply be a pause, as in an interlude or time to stop and reflect. Second, *Selah* might be derived from a Hebrew word meaning "to lift up," in which case it could mean to lift up one's voice to sing more loudly or to play an instrument more loudly. Third, it might derive from an Aramaic word for "to turn, to bend, or to pray," in which case it might be a cue for worshipers to kneel or bow before God.

Regardless of what you think *Selah* might mean, the traditional practice is simply to skip over this word whenever we read a psalm out loud. Similarly, I've chosen to ignore the *Selah* whenever it occurs in one of the psalms that I heart-learn.

Introduction to Hebrew Poetry

In the previous section, we took a broad look at the book of Psalms. We did a kind of "flyover" of the Psalms, noting a few of the landmarks in the terrain. These are helpful for understanding and appreciating the Psalms. But

---

7. Pemberton, *After Lament*, 83–84.
8. Griggs, *Psalms – Resource Book*, 10.

now we need to zoom down to a lower altitude and examine one of those characteristic landmarks in greater detail: Hebrew poetry.

Extra Steps:

Reflect on your attitude towards poetry. When you hear the word "poetry," what thoughts come to your mind? Did you like studying poetry in school? Do you enjoy reading poetry today? What do you like or not like about poetry?

Want to hear a confession? I have never really liked poetry all that much. Never. You start talking about poetry, and I'll tune you out very quickly. In my student days, we often had to study poetry in English literature classes, so I was exposed to the works of many great poets. We read and studied works by poets such as Robert Frost, e. e. cummings, Emily Dickinson, John Donne, and many others. But those poems never interested me all that much. I was always glad when the class moved on to some other topic.

Perhaps that's why the book of Psalms never interested me very much either. I've enjoyed studying the Bible for several decades now, but for most of that time, I much preferred the stories in the Gospels or the theological arguments in the writings of the Apostle Paul. I've also spent a lot of time learning about the Old Testament. But not the Psalms. I knew the Psalms weren't like the poetry I had been exposed to in all those English classes. That was obvious. But I think my dislike for English poetry fueled my lack of appreciation for the Psalms. I figured the Psalms were about as interesting as all those other poems I had read, which is to say, not very.

Looking back now, however, I believe my neglect of the Psalms was due in large measure to the fact that I understood so little about Hebrew poetry. In chapter 1 I told you how my new-found interest in the Psalms came about. Since then, as I've continued to work with the Psalms, I've discovered that I'm truly fascinated by Hebrew poetry. Hebrew poetry is radically different from the kinds of poetry I studied in school. You still won't find me reading a lot of English poems, but I've come to greatly value the poetry of the Psalms.

Now, you certainly don't need to be an expert on Hebrew poetry to appreciate the Psalms. On the other hand, C. S. Lewis warns that we also cannot ignore the poetical nature of the Psalms:

Most emphatically the Psalms must be read as poems; as lyrics, with all the licences and all the formalities, the hyperboles, the emotional rather than logical connections, which are proper to lyric poetry. They must be read as poems if they are to be understood; no less than French must be read as French or English as English. Otherwise, we shall miss what is in them and think we see what is not.[9]

So if we're going to understand the Psalms, we need at least some knowledge of how Hebrew poetry operates. That's what I'll be giving you in the following section. Even if you're a non-poetry-person like me, I'm confident you can still learn to appreciate the poetry of the Psalms.

Comparing English and Hebrew Poetry

As a literary form, all poetry communicates emotions and feelings in powerful ways. As N. T. Wright has observed, "A poem (a good poem, at least) uses its poetic form to probe deeper into human experience than ordinary speech or writing is usually able to do."[10] For this reason, although poetry certainly engages the mind, its ultimate target is the heart. Indeed, Frederick Buechner says that poetry "transcends all other language in its power to open the doors of the heart."[11] As it strives to reach our heart, poetry makes frequent use of images and metaphors to convey ideas and feelings, rather than resorting to lengthy explanations or narrative, as in prose. The use of imagery and metaphor is an important characteristic of both English and Hebrew poetry, and I'll examine this shortly. Before I do that, however, I'd like you to do the brief exercise described in this next "Extra Steps."

Extra Steps:

This exercise is intended to help you appreciate the difference between narrative and poetic accounts of the same event.[12] First, read Exodus 14:23–31, which recounts in story (or narrative) form God's

9. Lewis, *Reflections*, 3.
10. Wright, *Case for the Psalms*, 23.
11. Buechner, *Telling the Truth*, 21.
12. I am indebted to Tremper Longman III for this helpful comparison in his book, *How To Read the Psalms*, 91–92. His book also contains excellent chapters on Old Testament poetry, parallelism, and imagery. I learned much from his insightful explanations and descriptions.

> *destruction of the Egyptian armies and the deliverance of the Hebrews during their exodus from Egypt. Then, read the song of Moses in Exodus 15:1–12, which uses poetry to sing about the same event.*
>
> *In what ways do the two accounts differ? Do you prefer one account over the other? Why or why not? What are the strengths of each approach for helping you understand and appreciate God's act of delivering the Hebrew people?*

In addition to the use of imagery and metaphor, another characteristic of most poetry is that it's easier than prose to remember or memorize. This is equally true in both English and Hebrew poetry (and probably other languages as well). This explains why many of us can remember poems long after we first memorized them. They have a "stickiness" to them.

The major differences between English and Hebrew poetry are structural. In traditional English poetry, rhyme and rhythm are often central features. So we're accustomed to reading poetry with a certain beat (e.g., iambic pentameter), and we generally expect the sounds of the words to create a kind of music through rhyming or other poetical devices. However, Hebrew poetry uses neither rhythm nor rhyme. Instead, the distinguishing characteristic of Hebrew poetry is a concept called *parallelism*, which is a kind of thought-rhyming, where the thought in one line of the psalm (or poem) "rhymes" with the thought in the following line. Although this can look like mere repetition, it actually serves a much deeper purpose, which I'll explore with you shortly.

As a side note, since Hebrew poetry isn't based on rhyming words or rhythmic patterns, translating biblical psalms from Hebrew into English (or into any other language) is much easier than translating, say, French poetry into English. Trying to maintain the poetic rhythm when going from one language to another is very difficult, and finding the right words to rhyme without changing the meaning is often impossible. But translators of the Psalms face neither of those obstacles. As C. S. Lewis observed, "It is (according to one's point of view) either a wonderful piece of luck or a wise provision of God's that poetry which was to be turned into all languages should have as its chief formal characteristic one that does not disappear (as mere metre does) in translation."[13]

Before I take us into an exploration of parallelism, allow me to define a few basic terms.

13. Lewis, *Reflections*, 4–5.

Some Definitions in Hebrew Poetry

Line is the fundamental unit of Hebrew poetry. In some materials, a line may be referred to as a "stich" (a German word pronounced *stick*), with the plural being "stichs" (*sticks*). So, for example, Psalm 27:1, has two lines, or two stichs, even though it is printed using four physical lines in my Bible:

> Line 1: The Lord is my light and my salvation—whom shall I fear?
>
> Line 2: The Lord is the stronghold of my life—of whom shall I be afraid?

It's important to realize that a line (or stich) is not the same as a "verse." The verse numbers in our Bibles were added around 1200 AD—long after the biblical books were originally written. They're useful as references, but they're not part of the poetic structure in any of the psalms. Occasionally, the verse numbers can even be misleading. As an example of that, look at Psalm 19:4–5, where verse 5 obviously begins at the wrong place. This is one reason I've chosen not to memorize verse numbers as I heart-learn the Psalms. It's far more important to focus on the meaning of each psalm, and the verse numbers don't contribute to that understanding.

Another term is *strophe* (pronounced strō - fee), which is a grouping of lines (usually two or three) which are usually linked by some form of parallelism (I'll discuss this in the next section). The above example from Psalm 27:1 would be a strophe with two lines, which is the most common. Psalm 1:1 is an example of a strophe with three lines (although the *NIV* doesn't format it as such):

> Blessed is the one who does not walk in step with the wicked
> or stand in the way that sinners take
> or sit in the company of mockers

Strophes are often identical to the numbered verses in our Bibles, but you can't always rely on that. Much of our understanding of Hebrew poetry developed long after verse numbers began to be included in the text. As scholars have come to understand more about Hebrew poetry (especially the concept of parallelism), this has led to revisions in the translating and formatting of numerous psalms. However, in spite of these modern updates and corrections, the verse numbers have been left in their traditional locations. Not infrequently, this results in verse numbers being in the "wrong" place.

A third key term, *stanza*, refers to divisions within the psalm based on broad themes or ideas. One or more strophes may be grouped together into a stanza because they have a common theme, or because there's a major break in thought within the psalm. Stanzas are determined by the editors of the various translations and may vary from translation to translation. For instance, in my current Bible (the *NIV*), the editors have divided Psalm 27 into six stanzas (vss. 1, 2–3, 4–5, 6, 7–12, and 13–14). However, in my old 1978 version of the *NIV*, the same psalm had only four stanzas (vss. 1–3, 4–6, 7–12, and 13–14). This demonstrates how much stanza divisions are subject to editorial interpretation. Therefore, while they may be useful for understanding the flow of thought in the psalm, you may occasionally disagree with their placement, and that's perfectly legitimate.

Parallelism

As mentioned above, *parallelism* is the characteristic that truly sets Hebrew poetry apart. At first, we might be tempted to overlook it, thinking the poet/psalmist is simply repeating himself in a slightly different way for some unknown reason. Parallelism aids us in memorizing the Psalms, and it also helps with composing music for the Psalms, but John Witvliet points us to the real purpose in parallelism. He explains that "each slight alteration of the text helps us see a given reality in a new way—just as looking at an object with one eye and then with two eyes helps us perceive nuances and depth in an object."[14]

For this reason, learning about parallelism enables us to get more out of the Psalms, as we come to appreciate those nuances and depth in the biblical text more and more. As Alastair Hunter observes, "All poets are creative linguistic artists, and parallelism is part of the sheer pleasure of poetry."[15] We experience that pleasure—and increase our understanding and appreciation for the Psalms—when we grasp the basic concepts and types of parallelism.

I said earlier that parallelism is a kind of thought-rhyming. This rhyming of thoughts occurs in one of three basic ways:

---

14. Witvliet, *Psalms in Christian Worship*, 82.
15. Hunter, *Introduction to the Psalms*, 15.

(1) Synonymous Parallelism

In synonymous parallelism, one or two lines *repeat* the thought in the preceding line or lines but with different words. As an example, consider Psalm 84:2, where both lines say essentially the same thing but in different ways:

> My soul yearns, even faints, for the courts of the LORD;
> my heart and my flesh cry out for the living God.

Although the lines in synonymous parallelism repeat a thought or idea, this is not like a speaker simply repeating a sentence for some inattentive listener. Instead, the second line enriches the first by providing a slightly different way to view or think about something. In the above example, for instance, the second line makes the yearning for God physical. Both lines contain the same thought: the psalmist's deep desire to be in God's presence. However, if we had just the first line, we might think this longing occurs only in our inner being ("soul"). Adding the second line makes that longing physical as well ("my heart and my flesh"). Together, the two lines indicate that the psalmist hungers for God with his whole being. Neither line by itself is as rich as the two are together. This is the beauty of synonymous parallelism.

The concept of synonymous parallelism was illustrated for me one morning when Emma and I were walking in the nature preserve near our home. She was sniffing the ground, looking for the right place to do her "business," but I was stunned by the beautiful frost that covered the grass and bushes in the meadow where we were walking. As I waited for Emma, I pulled out my smartphone and used its built-in camera to capture the scene. However, I didn't take just one photo. I took several. One photo just wouldn't have done justice to the beauty before me. Each of the photos was similar—yet different. And together they portrayed the magnificence of that frosty morning. Synonymous parallelism does something quite similar. One line just isn't enough, so a second (and perhaps a third) line is added, similar to but slightly different from the first. Taken together, the lines shape an idea or image in our mind in a way that one line alone never could have.

(2) Antithetic Parallelism

With antithetic parallelism, an idea is repeated but the second line uses words or phrases that *contrast* with those in the first line. Psalm 1:6 provides a good example of this. The Lord's protection for the righteous is contrasted with the perishing of the wicked:

> For the LORD watches over the way of the righteous,
> but the way of the wicked leads to destruction.

What's important to see here, however, is that both of these lines are describing the same basic idea: that our destiny is determined by the path we choose to follow. The two lines make the same point, but they use words or phrases that have opposite meaning ("righteous"/"wicked" and "the LORD watches over"/"leads to destruction").

(3) Synthetic Parallelism

In synthetic parallelism, a new thought is *added* in the second line. The second line amplifies or expands on the first. Psalm 119:11 is an example of this:

> I have hidden your word in my heart
> that I might not sin against you.

In this strophe, the second line is not simply repeating the first line in a different way. Nor is it a contrast to the first line. Instead, the second line adds a new idea to the first line. In this case, it provides a purpose for hiding God's word in our heart. There are undoubtedly many reasons for hiding God's word in one's heart, but here the psalmist says he does so as a preventative measure against sin.

Psalm 1:1 provides an interesting variation of synthetic parallelism, often called a "staircase" form:

> Blessed is the one
> who does not walk in step with the wicked
> or stand in the way that sinners take
> or sit in the company of mockers.

Synthetic parallelism like these examples is extremely common in the Psalms. However, at least one Old Testament scholar thinks we should get rid of the synthetic category, arguing that it's really just a kind of "catchall" grouping for lines that are neither synonymous nor antithetic and that may not even be parallel at all.[16] This may well be correct, but most discussions of

---

16. Longman III, *Read the Psalms*, 100.

Hebrew parallelism include synthetic, along with synonymous and antithetical, as the three basic kinds of parallelism. So it's worth knowing about.

There are other forms of parallelism as well, some of which Longman also discusses, but these are the primary ones you should know about. In many cases, those other forms can be thought of as variations of these three primary forms. Regardless, it isn't critical to distinguish the precise type of parallelism at work in a particular strophe. What's important is for us to grasp the fundamental concept of parallelism and its thought-rhyming. As we learn to understand this feature in the text, we'll also come to love and appreciate the Psalms all the more.

Extra Steps:

Skim through several psalms and find examples of synonymous, antithetic, and synthetic parallelism. Reflect on a few of them. In each example, how does the parallelism enrich the overall idea in the strophe?

Imagery and Metaphor

Besides parallelism, another fundamental and important characteristic of Hebrew poetry (as well as English poetry) is the use of imagery and metaphor, which we'll look at in this section.

Psalm 84 has always been one of my favorites, and the *imagery* in verse 3 is one reason for this:

> Even the sparrow has found a home,
>   and the swallow a nest for herself,
>   where she may have her young—
> a place near your altar,
>   Lord Almighty, my King and my God.

Quite likely the psalmist had viewed some actual birds making nests in the upper corners and crevices of the temple in Jerusalem, just as we might see birds make a nest under the eaves of our home. Seeing those birds living in God's house made the psalmist a bit envious. He understood the wonderful privilege of being in God's presence. As he goes on to say in verse 4, "Blessed are those who dwell in your house; they are ever praising you."

When we're in God's presence, life is good. The imagery of these birds nesting in the temple reminds us of that.

I thought of this imagery the other day when I was out walking with Emma. I spotted a large hawk sitting high up in a tree, carefully surveying the ground below, and I wondered if that bird realized it's living in God's presence. Watching the hawk in its lofty perch, I said a brief prayer of thanks for the opportunity to be in God's presence as Emma and I walked along, to be on a holy walk with God himself.

Those birds in Psalm 84 and the hawk I observed on my walk are examples of *images*, and the Psalms are filled with images like that. Images are important because they work their way into our imaginations and have a power that goes well beyond that of mere description. So, for instance, the image of those birds creates mental pictures of what life is like when we're living in God's presence. Perhaps one could convey that idea in some other way, but this image does so very powerfully.

Images also enable us to talk about concepts that seem to defy description. For instance, take a moment and think how you would describe God's glory. Rather hard, isn't it? But the psalmist looks up at the sky and says, "The heavens declare the glory of God" (Ps. 19:1). He uses the image of the sky ("the heavens") to help us understand something of God's glory. On many occasions a spectacular sunrise has caused me to pray the words of Psalm 8:1, "You have set your glory in the heavens." I may not be able to describe God's glory very well, but when I look at the spectacular colors and clouds of a beautiful sunrise, I know I've seen the glory of God.

An image becomes a *metaphor* when it's compared to something else, such as when the psalmist refers to God as a rock. There's no literal connection between God and a rock, but the psalmist uses the image of a rock as a metaphor in order to say something about God. He takes an image from the everyday world and uses it as an analogy for something that goes beyond the image itself. That's what metaphors do. When the psalmist makes that comparison explicit by using "like" or "as," we call it a *simile*. So "the Lord is my shepherd" (Ps. 23:1) is a metaphor, but "the life of mortals is like grass" (Ps. 103:15) is a simile. Functionally, similes are a kind of metaphor and have the same purpose.

So, when David uses the metaphor, "The Lord is my shepherd," he isn't saying that God is actually a shepherd. Rather, he's saying there's some kind of correspondence between God and human shepherds—God has some of the same qualities as we see in a shepherd—and so we learn something about God by looking at the way a shepherd cares for his sheep. David, of course, describes many of those points of similarity in the rest of this deeply-loved psalm.

Similarly, when a psalmist refers to God as a "Rock," he isn't saying that God is literally a rock (something a polytheist might say). Instead, he's thinking of God's strength or permanence, ideas that are conveyed by the image of a rock. We can truthfully describe God as being strong and eternal, but how much more powerful is it to say that God is a Rock?

However, images and metaphors also have limitations. As John Witvliet points out, metaphors "both lie and tell the truth."[17] For instance, when a psalm says that God is a rock, it's certainly telling us something truthful, namely that God is incredibly strong and permanent and therefore reliable. But it's also "lying" because God is not lifeless, as the rock is. When we encounter images or metaphors in a psalm, it's important to understand the point of comparison, but we must also avoid pushing the metaphor too far, lest it says something that was never intended. For instance, when a psalm refers to God's people as "sheep," we hope it isn't saying that you and I are smelly and dumb like sheep!

To help us understand more about images, metaphors, and similes, let's look at some examples in Psalm 92. Take a moment and read through this psalm, noticing the various images and metaphors. I'll wait for you.

* * *

Here are some of the images you might have noticed:

1. In verse 4 we have an example of *personification*: "I sing for joy at what your hands have done." Obviously, God doesn't really have hands, but in speaking of God's activity in the world, the psalmist speaks as though he does. That's personification, which is a form of metaphor. Rivers clapping their hands and mountains leaping for joy (see, e.g., Ps. 98:8) are other examples of personification.

2. We have an example of a *simile* in verse 7: "the wicked spring up like grass." The word "like" tells us it's a simile rather than a metaphor. With this simile the psalmist conveys the idea that godless people seem to be everywhere and that more of them appear all the time. But he goes on to affirm that this will not always be the case and that, eventually, the wicked will be subject to God's judgment.

---

17. Witvliet, *Psalms in Christian Worship*, 17.

3. Verse 10 contains *images* that are more difficult for many of us to immediately appreciate: "You have exalted my horn like that of a wild ox; fine oils have been poured on me." This is a reminder that images in the Psalms are always drawn from the psalmists' culture, not ours. Most of the time this isn't a problem, but in this instance, horns, wild oxen, and having oil poured on us may not produce the kind of mental picture the psalmist intended. In such cases, consulting a good commentary can be helpful. There you would find that "horn" is often a symbol of strength and energy and "fine oils" were essentially skin moisturizers, extremely valuable in the hot, dry climate of the Middle East.[18] You may also find it useful to consult Eugene Peterson's *The Message*, since he renders many of the biblical images into more contemporary ones. For example, he renders this verse, "But you've made me strong as a charging bison, you've honored me with a festive parade." That may be a much more understandable imagery.

4. Verse 12 contains another *simile*, actually two of them used in parallel: "The righteous will flourish like a palm tree, they will grow like a cedar of Lebanon." We don't have palm trees where I live, and we certainly don't have any Lebanese cedars either. But we're all familiar enough with these images to understand the point of the simile—and also to see the contrast with the "wicked" who are compared to "grass." Palm trees are tall and luxuriant, and the cedars of Lebanon were prized for being strong and tall. Think of how different this image would be if the righteous were compared to an ornamental cherry tree, or a saguaro cactus, or a tumbleweed. Finding the right image makes all the difference.

5. The following verse, verse 13, elaborates on that flourishing of the righteous by adding, "They will still bear fruit in old age, they will stay fresh and green." Instead of going barren and withering like plants do as they age, the righteous will continue to be fruitful and filled with growth and health, at least in a spiritual sense. As one who is approaching "old age" in the calendar-sense, I find this *image* especially encouraging.

6. Verse 15 contains another of those "the Lord is my Rock" *metaphors*. Here the point is that God is the solid foundation for the righteous as they go through life. As they age, they change, but, like a rock, God doesn't. This final verse also says, "The Lord is upright," and

---

18. Longman III, *Psalms* (TOTC), 333.

that sounds like a metaphor, similar to "the Lord is my Rock." However, "The LORD is upright" is a simple statement of fact rather than a metaphor. Unlike with the rock, there's no comparison involved. The psalmist is simply declaring that God is righteous or moral. Thus, there's no metaphor involved.

I chose this particular psalm for us to look at because of the number and variety of images, similes, and metaphors in it. As you continue to work with the Psalms, learn to watch for images like these, and then take some time to reflect on how the image (or simile or metaphor) enriches your thoughts. Grasping the meaning of the imagery and metaphors is vital if we're going to understand the various messages and teachings of the Psalms.

Extra Steps:

Think of an image, simile, or metaphor for each of the following theological concepts: love, mercy, compassion, grace, holiness, righteousness, sin, judgment, salvation. Here's an example to get you started: "God loves us like a mother embracing her newborn baby for the first time." What others can you think of?

Acrostic Psalms

One special (and fun) kind of Hebrew poetry is the *acrostic psalm*. In an acrostic psalm, the first letters of each line form some sort of pattern. For example, in Psalm 145, each strophe begins with a different Hebrew letter, in consecutive order from *aleph* (the first letter in the Hebrew alphabet) through *taw* (the twenty-second and last letter in the Hebrew alphabet). Since this is a psalm of praise, we might say that the psalmist is praising God from A to Z.

Perhaps the most well-known example of an acrostic psalm is Psalm 119. In this very long psalm (176 verses), all eight lines in each stanza begin with the same Hebrew letter, starting with *aleph* in the first stanza, *beth* (the second Hebrew letter) in the second stanza, and going through *taw* in the final (twenty-second) stanza. The *NIV* editors have placed the appropriate Hebrew letter above each of the stanzas to help you appreciate this feature.

Other acrostic psalms include Psalms 9, 10, 25, 34, 37, 111, and 112. Unfortunately, this feature is only apparent in the Hebrew text. For that reason, when I teach this topic in classes, I frequently bring my Hebrew Bible and let people view the text. Even without knowing any Hebrew, they can see the repetition of Hebrew letters at the beginning of the lines in Psalm 119 or one of the other acrostic psalms.

We can only speculate on the purpose behind acrostic psalms. The psalmists may have resorted to the acrostic methodology as an aid for memorizing these psalms. That may indeed be a side benefit, but C. S. Lewis points out that the technique of writing an acrostic poem "is a pattern, a thing done like embroidery, stitch by stitch, through long, quiet hours, for love of the subject and for the delight in leisurely, disciplined craftsmanship."[19] So my theory is that the writers of the acrostic psalms viewed it as a special way to shape their prayers and praises to the God who created the heavens and the earth in such special ways. Creating an acrostic poem requires extra effort. Perhaps these psalms were the psalmists' way to offer a little extra to God.

Extra Steps:

Try writing your own acrostic psalm of praise to God. And, no, you don't have to do it in Hebrew! Instead, the first line should begin with the letter A, the second with B, the third with C, and so forth. Or you can come up with your own pattern. But remember that you don't need to worry about rhyming or meter. Try to include some imagery or parallelism if you can.

Here are a few sample lines to get you started (although I'm sure you can do much better):

All *the world is your footstool, O Lord!*

By *Your power the earth spins in space;*

Creation looks to you for direction and provision;

Now keep going with **D** *through* **Z** *...*

---

19. Lewis, *Reflections*, 58–59.

Chapter 6

Rain or Shine, You Gotta Go Out!

"Let the morning bring me word of your unfailing love,
for I have put my trust in you.
Show me the way I should go,
for to you I entrust my life."

—Psalm 143:8

The Psalms as Prayers for Every Day

Emma is snoozing in her favorite chair near the window when I utter the magic word: "Walk!" She's getting a little hard of hearing now, so I have to repeat it, a little more loudly this time: *"WALK!"* This time she sits up, her ears tilt forward, and her face brightens. She loves to go for walks, and she's clearly excited. However, before she jumps out of the chair, she turns and takes a quick glance out the window. I can't be sure, but I suspect she's doing a weather check. She's wondering, "What's the weather like outside?" With her meteorological curiosity apparently satisfied, she turns her attention back to me and quickly trots over so I can put the leash on her. We're about to set off on another holy walk.

I love taking Emma for walks when it's seventy-five degrees out and the sun is shining brightly in a clear, blue sky. Add in the beautiful colors of a fall day, and walking the dog doesn't get much better than that. But, unfortunately, not all days are like that. In eastern Washington where I now live, we get our share of rainy days, and winter days are usually frigid and snowy. Walking Emma on some of those days isn't much fun. But she still has to go out—rain or shine! So no matter what the weather's like, every day we still head out on our walks.

Just as the days bring many kinds of weather, so there are many kinds of psalms. In Michigan, where I used to live, people would often say to me, "If you don't like the weather, wait five minutes, and it'll change!" A similar saying for the book of Psalms might go like this: "If you don't like the psalm you're reading right now, read another couple minutes and you'll be reading a very different kind of psalm."

Indeed, even a superficial reading of the Psalms reveals great differences in style and emotional feel. There are psalms for those days when we feel especially happy or blessed or thankful. Some are good for those days when we're in a reflective mood. A surprisingly large number of psalms are written for those days when we feel like life is falling apart. And, finally, some psalms simply express our faith and trust in God and fit with whatever the weather is like in our lives. Because of this incredible variety, I like to think of the psalms as *prayers for every day*. No matter what my day is like, there are psalms that speak to me and for me.

Biblical scholars have long recognized that there are different kinds, or *types*, of psalms. They've examined the psalms in great detail, trying to determine the original purpose for each psalm and to categorize them accordingly. Writing in the early part of the twentieth century, the German scholar, Hermann Gunkel, was the first to propose a typology for the psalms. He argued that the psalms could be divided into six main types: Hymns of Praise, Enthronement Psalms, Laments of the Community, Individual Songs of Thanksgiving, Laments of the Individual, and Royal Psalms. Later, another influential scholar, Claus Westermann, suggested that every psalm is either a song of praise or a lament. Walter Brueggemann, a contemporary Old Testament scholar, takes a slightly different approach. He categorizes each of the psalms as falling into one of three types: Psalms of Orientation, Psalms of Disorientation, and Psalms of New Orientation.[1] In his teaching materials on the Psalms, Donald Griggs follows *The New Oxford Annotated Bible: NRSV* in identifying ten different types of psalms: hymns of praise, enthronement hymns, songs of Zion, psalms of lament, songs of trust, sacred history psalms, royal psalms, songs of thanksgiving, wisdom psalms,

---

1. Brueggemann, *Message of the Psalms*. In March 2013 I had the great privilege of participating in a small workshop led by Dr. Brueggemann. Among the topics we discussed were these three types of psalms.

and liturgies.[2] Another contemporary scholar, Bernhard Anderson, recognizes seventeen types.[3] Clearly, there's no scholarly consensus regarding a typology of the Psalms.

As I've worked with the Psalms and considered what the scholars have written, I've found it helpful to divide the psalms into five primary types. I freely acknowledge that some psalms may not fit easily into any of these five categories, and certainly many psalms exhibit characteristics of more than one type. Nevertheless, I believe there's value in focusing on these five types:

1. *Psalms of Trust* are expressions of trust, faith, or confidence in God. These are often very personal and inspiring, and, for that reason, whenever I ask people to name their favorite psalm, they most often cite a Psalm of Trust, with Psalm 23, the Shepherd Psalm, leading the way by far. Although this is the most familiar and beloved psalm today, it did not achieve such popularity until late in the nineteenth century, when a well-known preacher of that day, Henry Ward Beecher, extolled its virtues. Beecher (1813–1887) wrote, "The twenty-third psalm is the nightingale of the psalms. It is small, of a homely feather, singing shyly out of obscurity; but, O, it has filled the air of the whole world with melodious joy, greater than the heart can conceive."[4] Psalm 23 may have been "singing shyly out of obscurity" for many centuries, but today it's a wonderful example of a Psalm of Trust.

2. *Wisdom Psalms* are generalized observations about the way life "works." The book of Proverbs is a familiar example of wisdom literature, with its collection of sayings, adages, and exhortations. Wisdom literature commonly uses strong contrasts and cause-and-effect phrasing, like we see in Proverbs. Another frequent feature of the Wisdom Psalms is a stress on obedience to the Law, or *Torah*. In fact, they're sometimes

---

2. Griggs, *Psalms – Resource Book*, 10. Although I have not followed Griggs in my typology of the psalms, I do find his teaching materials on the Psalms to be excellent, and I've drawn extensively on them. His *Resource Book* and *Leader's Guide* are clear and easily accessible to anyone who wants to learn more about the Psalms. Kerygma, in general, produces outstanding materials for adult education in the church, and I highly recommend them.

3. Anderson assigns one of his seventeen types to each of the 150 psalms in an index in *Out of the Depths*, 219–24. He acknowledges, however, that it's impossible to be certain of the typology for many psalms.

4. Pemberton, *After Lament*, 79. Pemberton discusses other reasons as well for the growth in popularity of Psalm 23.

called *Torah* Psalms. These psalms present obedience to the Law as the key to God's blessing in life. Psalm 1 is a good example of this.

3. *Sacred Story Psalms* are lengthy rehearsals of how God has led and worked with his people throughout their history. Psalm 78 is one example of this type of psalm. When we first encounter one of these psalms, we're probably tempted to skim through it (or skip it altogether), because it doesn't seem especially relevant to our life today. But I believe these psalms serve a valuable purpose for us, as I'll discuss shortly.

4. *Psalms of Lament* are emotional responses to the sin, suffering, and injustice that we experience in life. These psalms often contain the rawest of emotions, including anger, feelings of persecution, abandonment, or betrayal, and a desire for vengeance. Psalm 13 is a powerful example of a lament, but there are many others. Many Christians are perplexed by the Psalms of Lament and don't quite know what to do with them. They seem to go against much of the teaching in the New Testament, and at times they even seem almost un-Christian. But, properly understood, these psalms are precisely what we need in order to strengthen our faith during life's most difficult times, as I'll show in the next chapter.

5. *Psalms of Praise* are poems honoring and glorifying God for who God is and what God's done. Psalm 145 is a wonderful example of a praise psalm, although there are many others. Indeed, most psalms (including the laments) include some aspect of praise to God. However, even when a particular psalm contains praises to God, if it fits into one of the other four types, that's the type I consider it to be. To be classified as a Psalm of Praise, the central intent of the psalm needs to be praise to God for who God is or what God's done.

Extra Steps:

Take a few minutes to skim through the following psalms and place each of them into one of the five types described above:

Psalms 12, 30, 42, 66, 105, 111, 119, and 121

Try to identify why you classified each of them the way you did. What words, phrases, or verses helped you determine the type?

> *(I'll provide you with my answers to this exercise at the end of the chapter. However, the point is not to get them "right" but to begin cultivating an awareness of the different types of psalms.)*

In spite of the disagreements about the types of psalms, attempting to classify them is still valuable, because it helps us think about the various purposes for the psalms. Indeed, I believe a major reason for the popularity of the book of Psalms is precisely this variety of purposes. No matter what any given day of ours is like—sunny, rainy, windy, foggy, overcast, snowy—no matter what we're going through, there's a psalm that expresses our feelings and puts our thoughts into words. There truly is a psalm for every day, and the Psalms really are prayers for every day. Knowing about the different types of psalms enables us to appreciate this truth all the more clearly.

For biblical scholars, categorizing the psalms by type is generally a way to explore the original usages of the psalms in the individual and communal lives of the ancient Israelites. While this may have value in academic circles, my concern is more with how God wishes to use the psalms in the lives of people today. The original purpose of any given psalm is not irrelevant in that contemporary use, but neither is it the final word. God can and will use *each* of the psalms in our lives, even if the original purpose does not appear to fit the context of life here in the twenty-first century.

Understanding the different types of psalms is important for another reason as well. In my work with the Psalms, I've come to believe that, as I recite the words of a psalm in a faith-filled prayer to God, God graciously speaks those same words into my heart. Prayer is never just me speaking to God—although we often view prayer that way. Rather, prayer is always a dialogue or a conversation (as I discussed in chapter 4), and as the words of the psalmist become my words, they also become words that God speaks to me. And God's words usually address me in different ways, depending on the type of psalm I'm praying.

Thus, *Psalms of Trust* strengthen my faith and inspire me to live more fully for God. They can carry me through crises and challenging times of life. *Wisdom Psalms* remind me of the importance of obedience to God's law, teachings, and ways. They direct me to listen to God's Word (not only the Psalms but the rest of the Bible as well) and to strive to live a life that is pleasing to the Lord. *Sacred Story Psalms* connect me with my spiritual heritage and help me see myself as part of the larger family of God's people and the Great Story that God is working out in history. *Psalms of Lament* are vehicles for me to bring my complaints, worries, and fears to God, which then opens me to God's peace and healing grace. And, finally, *Psalms of Praise* are a way for me to express my wonder, gratitude, and love to God and to experience more of God's love in return.

So as I pray these different types of psalms to God, I believe God works in different ways in my heart. Of course, God is quite free to work in any way he desires through any of the psalms, but it seems to me this is one explanation for why God has chosen to give us so much variety in the book of Psalms.

With that awareness for why we're dividing the psalms into these five types, let's dive in more deeply and examine each of those types. I'll discuss the first three types in the remainder of this chapter, and then I'll consider the other two in the next two chapters.

Psalms of Trust

Emma is a wonderful dog and a faithful walking companion. She's incredibly gentle, loves people, and would never hurt a fly. A squirrel maybe, but she's never caught one yet, so I can't be sure. However, in spite of all her good qualities, I know better than to trust her in one particular area. That area is anything to do with food. Simply put, Emma is a food thief. If Carol or I leave any food where Emma can get to it, well, it won't be there for long!

We were reminded of this one time when we were getting ready to go to a church potluck. We had been assigned to bring a dessert, and so we had picked up a beautiful blueberry pie to take along as our contribution. I love fruit pies, and I was already plotting how I could be sure of getting a slice for myself. Carol had placed the pie on the kitchen counter, and we were in the back of the house, finishing getting dressed.

Suddenly, we heard strange noises from the kitchen and hurried out to see what was going on. We were met with the sight of blueberry filling all over the kitchen. On the floor, on the cabinets, on the counter. Everywhere. Somehow, Emma had managed to reach the pie with her paw and pull it close enough so she could get her mouth in it. Then, with pure delight, I'm sure, she had flung blueberry pie all around. Evidently, she really likes blueberry!

So Carol and I learned our lesson that day: Never, never trust Emma when it comes to food.

Trust is an essential quality in any relationship, isn't it? Indeed, the degree of trust often reveals the nature and strength of a relationship. When I have a strong relationship with someone, it shows in the ways I trust that person. The opposite is also true. Whenever there's a lack of trust in a relationship, the relationship is diminished because of it. So building trust is essential if we're going to have a deep and vibrant relationship with someone.

For that reason, trust is also essential in our relationship with God. Trust may go by many other words, such as faith, hope, or confidence, but without trust, we won't have much of a relationship with God. In fact, we might even say that, without trust, we won't have *any* relationship with God. Similarly, the more we trust God, the stronger our relationship with God will be.

Perhaps this is why trust in God is such a major theme in the book of Psalms. We see that on a simple level, for instance, in the personal expression, "my God," which is found throughout the Psalms. Addressing God in that way certainly indicates at least some measure of trust. In addition, Donald Griggs points out that the actual word "trust" appears in some form in thirty-two psalms (forty-two total verses), and he concludes that trust "is the single dominant theme in the whole book."[5]

While this emphasis on trust can be found throughout the book of Psalms, there are at least a dozen psalms that can be categorized as Psalms of Trust. These include Psalms 4, 11, 16, 23, 26, 27, 62, 63, 91, 121, 131, and 146. In each of these psalms, the psalmists are declaring their personal trust in God in some way. These are personal affirmations of the psalmists' faith and confidence in God to protect, deliver, or save them. Certainly, these psalms also contain praise and thanksgiving for God, and they sometimes contain lament as well. However, the central idea of each of these psalms is the psalmist's trust in God, and that's what puts them in this category.

Let's examine one of those Psalms of Trust, Psalm 16, and see if we can understand why it fits into this type of psalm. So get out your Bible and take a moment to read through this psalm. I'll wait for you. . . .

Extra Steps:

As you read Psalm 16, reflect on these questions:

What acts or actions of God are mentioned in the psalm?

5. Griggs, *Psalms – Resource Book*, 59.

RAIN OR SHINE, YOU GOTTA GO OUT!

How does David respond to those actions on God's part?

Which words or phrases demonstrate David's trust in God?

I was first drawn to Psalm 16 because of the gratitude that David[6] expresses for how God has worked in his life. As I understand the psalm, it sounds like David is perhaps getting up in years and is looking back on his life with gratitude for all that God has done for him. That's something I can be pretty blind to in my own life, and reading this psalm moved me to want to become more like David. As I get older, I don't want to become a grumpy old guy—there are already too many of those around as it is. Rather, I want to be more thankful to God for all that God's done for me throughout my life. So I started heart-learning this psalm a few years ago, and it's been one of my regular prayers ever since. (I can still be grumpy at times—just ask Carol—so I better keep on praying this psalm!)

Even though Psalm 16 has obvious elements of praise and thanksgiving, I still see it as a Psalm of Trust. Why is that?

The first clue is in the opening verse. David says he takes "refuge" in God. A refuge is a place of safety and security. For the ancient Israelites, "cities of refuge" were places where a person could flee for safety from someone who was seeking to avenge the death of a relative.[7] In Psalm 16, David views God as a city of refuge, a place of safety from the dangers of the world around him. So he begins this psalm by declaring that he trusts that God will keep him safe.

Along with "refuge," Psalms of Trust often characterize God as being a "fortress," a "stronghold," a "shelter," or a "tent." Each of these metaphors indicates that God is a place of security and that God protects us and keeps us safe. The metaphor of God as a Rock is also used frequently to indicate God's power and reliability, another reason why we can trust God. The familiar image of God as a Shepherd in Psalm 23 (and other psalms as well) is yet another metaphor to indicate trust. God's people can trust God in the same way that sheep can trust their shepherd. Additional images of trust include being in the shadow of God's wings (Psalm 63:7) and being

---

6. For the issue of the authorship of the various psalms, see the discussion in chapter 5. I find it simpler to refer to David as the author of psalms like this one, even though I'm fully aware of the ambiguity in the phrase "of David" in the superscriptions of various psalms.

7. See, e.g., Exod. 21:12–14, Num. 35:6–34, and Josh. 20:1–9.

a weaned child in the arms of his or her mother (Psalm 131:2). Of course, there are many others as well.

Another clue that Psalm 16 is a Psalm of Trust is seen in David's numerous declarations of his own personal confidence in God. For instance, in verse 2 he expresses his complete dependence on God: "I say to the Lord, 'You are my Lord; apart from you I have no good thing.'" In verse 5 he says, "Lord, you alone are my portion and my cup; you make my lot secure." In verse 8, he writes, "I keep my eyes always on the Lord. With him at my right hand, I will not be shaken." And, finally, in verses 10 and 11, he confidently declares that God won't "abandon me to the realm of the dead" but "will fill me with joy in your presence, with eternal pleasures at your right hand." David knows he can trust God even in the face of death.

Thus, we see that Psalm 16 is a confident and assured declaration of David's trust in God. Over the years, God has proven himself to be trustworthy for David in all kinds of ways. Now David is affirming his complete trust in God.

Psalms of Trust, like Psalm 16, are a kind of confession of faith, but not in the way of a creedal confession. When we recite the Apostles' Creed or the Nicene Creed, we're confessing our faith and declaring what we believe. But those are primarily *doctrinal* declarations. Psalms of Trust testify to the psalmist's *personal* trust and faith in God. Reciting a creed reminds us of important theological truths and strengthens our commitment to those beliefs, but the purpose of the Psalms of Trust is to strengthen our trust in God.

Today, many of us trust in all sorts of things to protect us, keep us safe, bring us a sense of personal fulfillment, or help us flourish and prosper. We put our trust in weapons, money, government, doctors, friends, or ourselves. Things such as those can be good, of course, but, like my dog Emma with blueberry pie, none of them is worthy of our complete trust. All of those things will let us down in some way at some time.

Only God is trustworthy in every area of life, without question and without limitation. And the Psalms of Trust, especially, remind us of that critical fact of life. As we pray these psalms, and as they become part of our heart, we learn to trust God more and more. Heart-learning and praying these psalms builds, strengthens, and deepens our trust in God. So I keep on praying the words of Psalm 16 (and others), believing that as David's words of trust in God are formed on my lips, they're also taking form in my heart. And I invite you to do the same with these Psalms of Trust.

Extra Steps:

Here's a great prayer activity to do with a small group. Ask the people to take about five minutes to skim through various psalms at random. Tell them to look for verses that reflect trust, confidence, faith, or hope in God. At the end of the five minutes, ask each person to select one or two of those verses which are especially meaningful to him or her. Then have a time of corporate prayer during which each person simply reads one of the verses they selected. Ask them not to cite the reference; just read the verse without introduction or comment. After a verse is read, the group responds in unison: "Praise the Lord!" Then the next verse is read, and the group responds again with "Praise the Lord!" Continue that way until all the verses have been read. Then simply close with "Amen."

Wisdom Psalms

Psalms of Trust are an important type of psalm. Another key type is Wisdom Psalms, which I'll discuss in this section. To see some of the characteristics of Wisdom Psalms, take a few moments and read through Psalm 1. As you read it, ask yourself this question: *Is this psalm a prayer?*

* * *

So what did you decide? Is Psalm 1 a prayer? In favor of a "yes" answer is the fact that it's included in the book of Psalms, which we've been referring to as God's Prayer Book. But arguing for a "no" answer is the fact that the psalm doesn't address God or ask God for anything, two elements that we normally associate with prayer. So which is it? Prayer or not a prayer? Hold onto that question for a few more moments while I present some additional background for Psalm 1.

Psalm 1 exhibits characteristics of a type of writing that biblical scholars refer to as wisdom literature. The Bible, of course, contains numerous types, or genres, of writing, and wisdom literature is only one of those. A few other types include historical narratives (e.g., Judges or 1 and 2 Kings), gospel narratives (such as Matthew), epistles (like Paul's letters), and apocalyptic (Revelation and parts of Daniel and Ezekiel). The book of Proverbs is probably the best-known example of wisdom literature, although the books of Job and Ecclesiastes are two others.

In the New Testament, the letter of James is widely regarded as having the form of wisdom literature. To see why this is, compare the letter of James to any of the Apostle Paul's letters. As letters, James and Paul's writings will have similarities in their form, but Paul relies on logical arguments as he teaches his intended audience, while James draws, in large measure, on popular sayings and commonly accepted facts and observations about life. He also jumps from one topic to another, often with no apparent reason (the book of Proverbs also does that). This makes it relatively simple to develop an outline for a Pauline letter but a real challenge with the letter of James (as it is with the book of Proverbs).

Two central features distinguish wisdom literature from other kinds of writing:

First of all, a primary characteristic of wisdom literature is the use of *sharp contrasts*. Here in Psalm 1, for instance, we have contrasts between the wicked and the righteous, the way of the wicked and the way of the righteous, and the judgment of the wicked and the prosperity of the righteous. Now you and I both realize that life is not nearly as black-and-white as that: people are not so easily classified, the "way" is not always so clearly marked, and judgment/prosperity is not so absolute (in this life at least). But wisdom writing speaks in polar-opposite contrasts like that in order to make a point.

Wisdom literature is also marked, secondly, by *broad generalizations* about the way life "works," especially when it comes to the consequences of different behaviors. The wisdom writers base their teaching on careful observations and reflections about the way life usually seems to operate. This experiential nature of wisdom writing contrasts with the prophetic methodology, in which the prophets receive words directly from God himself to speak to the people. So, while the prophets declare, "Thus says the Lord!," the wisdom writers make statements like, "If you do X, then good things will happen, but if you do Y, then bad things will happen." Of course, these wisdom writers are just as inspired as the prophets. The Spirit's inspiration simply takes a different form when it comes to the wisdom writings.

In Psalm 1 we see this second characteristic of wisdom literature in the blessing that's enjoyed by persons who don't follow the sinful ways of people around them. Once again, the picture in Psalm 1 is very black-and-white. If you walk in the right ways (avoiding the sinful ways and obeying

God's law), then you'll be blessed and the Lord will watch over you. But if you don't, then you'll be blown away like chaff in the wind and face the judgment of God. There's very little middle ground in wisdom literature. Either you do or you don't. It's important to remember that these are true statements about life *in general*, even though we can all cite examples of wicked or sinful people who have prospered and godly saints who have gone bankrupt. Wisdom literature is based on broad experience and observations about the way life *generally* works.

A related characteristic that we often see in wisdom literature is an emphasis on obedience to God's law, or the *Torah*. Wisdom writing is always concerned with how people should live and how they can enjoy the blessing of God for a life well lived. The biblical writers recognize that God's law is a vital source for obtaining wisdom, and obedience to the law brings blessing and reward, just as disobedience brings judgment and destruction. Psalm 1 highlights this characteristic by describing the blessed person as one "whose delight is in the law of the Lord, and who meditates on his law day and night" (v. 2).

Wisdom writings are not limited to ancient literature. For instance, Benjamin Franklin is famous for his many wisdom sayings, such as, "A penny saved is a penny earned" and "Three may keep a secret, if two of them are dead." We have plenty of wisdom sayings floating around today as well. In fact, your parents probably resorted to some of them in raising you. I remember my mom often saying, "Don't go swimming right after you eat, or you'll get cramps!" and "Put a coat on, so you don't catch a cold!" I don't know why those two bits of "wisdom" stuck with me all these years, but they did.

Here's an example of another wisdom saying I heard not too long ago:

> What's the difference between cats and dogs? A cat says, "You feed me, you pet me, you love me. I must be God!" A dog says, "You feed me, you pet me, you love me. You must be God!"

That saying isn't a prophetic declaration, nor is it an example of rational, didactic teaching. It's wisdom writing. It says there are two kinds of people in the world, those who worship God and those who worship themselves, and it forces us to consider which kind we are. That's the way wisdom stories and wisdom sayings work. They're not promises. They're not scientific formulas. They're simply generalized reflections about life, based on broad experiences and numerous observations. (As a dog-lover, I had to include that story. And, if you're a cat-lover, well, maybe you should consider getting a dog!)

From this overview of wisdom literature and these examples of wisdom sayings and stories, you can see why Psalm 1 is considered to be a Wisdom Psalm. However, it's certainly not the only one of this type, and several other psalms can also be classified as Wisdom Psalms, including Psalms 37, 49, 73, 112, 127, 128, and 133. I believe we should also include psalms that focus on the Law (*Torah* Psalms) as Wisdom Psalms.[8] So this adds Psalms 19 and 119 to the list.

Occasionally, we'll also find wisdom sayings within psalms that would more accurately belong to a different type. For example, verse 5 in Psalm 30 is clearly a wisdom saying:

> For his anger lasts only a moment,
>   but his favor lasts a lifetime;
> weeping may stay for the night,
>   but rejoicing comes in the morning.

Yet, overall, Psalm 30 is not a Wisdom Psalm; it would be better classified as either a Psalm of Trust or a Praise Psalm. Remember that the psalm type is determined by the *overall* emphasis or form within each psalm, even though the psalm may contain elements of other types. This holds true for all five types of psalms that we're examining.

Extra Steps:

Psalm 127 is generally classified as a Wisdom Psalm. It's attributed to Solomon, who was known for his great wisdom, so the psalm was likely written either by Solomon himself or by someone else in honor of Solomon and his wisdom. Besides the authorship attribution, what features in this psalm cause it to be listed as a Wisdom Psalm?

How many different topics are addressed in these five verses?

What wisdom teaching is provided in each of those topics?[9]

---

8. Donald Griggs also does this in his teaching materials. See *Psalms – Resource Book*, 13.

9. Glenn Pemberton has an excellent discussion of this psalm in his book, *After Lament*, 158–61. He shows how the psalm addresses the folly in our natural desire to believe we're in charge of our lives.

Let's go back now to the question I posed at the beginning of this section: *Is Psalm 1 a prayer?* Allow me to answer by describing my own experience with this psalm.

I begin many of my holy walks by praying Psalm 1. As Emma and I head down the driveway on our way to the park (or wherever our destination might be), I offer the words of Psalm 1 up to God: "Blessed is the one . . . who meditates on his law day and night . . . That person is like a tree [perhaps a Ponderosa pine?] planted by streams of water . . . Whatever they do prospers . . . The LORD watches over the way of the righteous." As I recite the psalm, my words don't take the form of a traditional prayer. I don't invoke God's presence or ask God to hear me. I simply offer God the words of Psalm 1 as a prayer from my heart.

So, is Psalm 1 a prayer? Perhaps not in its original form and usage. Many commentators have observed that Psalm 1 (and usually Psalm 2 as well) serves as a kind of introduction to the entire book of Psalms. At some point during the long process in which the Psalms were compiled into the collection we have now, Psalm 1 was intentionally chosen to be the first among the 150 psalms. When we view the psalm only from that perspective, it doesn't appear to be a prayer. But for me, it's a prayer that God will shape me into someone who is like the blessed person in Psalm 1, someone who walks in God's ways, who delights in God's Word, and who's fruitful and prosperous in the ways God desires me to be. Praying Wisdom Psalms like that is my way of telling God that I truly want to walk in his ways and asking him to give me the wisdom necessary for doing so.

In my early days of following Jesus, I was told that "a good Christian doesn't smoke or dance or go with girls that do." Later, I was taught that "good" Christians have a Daily Quiet Time, give ten percent of their income to God's work (tithe), and always pray before meals, even in restaurants. Many years later, I learned that "good" Christians don't mow their lawns or wash their cars on Sundays. I even got called out once for doing some grocery shopping on a Sunday afternoon—evidently another Sabbath violation.

Much of Christianity today is based on rules like those. (Perhaps you can think of a few rules that your Christian community adheres to.) The problem with rules, however, is that you can never have a rule for every situation. Plus, rule-keeping easily turns us into Pharisees: "I keep the rules better than you do!" Keeping rules may be a helpful starting place for young believers, just as it is for young children. But if we're going to follow God faithfully and obediently in a complex and ever-changing world, we need something more than rule-keeping. We need wisdom.

Wisdom is the ability to apply God's values and commands to life today, to take the teachings of the Bible and apply them in our everyday living. We need wisdom to guide us if we're going to apply the stories and commands in the Scriptures to the varied situations we encounter in life. Even biblical commands that appear to be straightforward can be difficult to apply. For example, in Exodus 20:13 the sixth commandment succinctly declares, "You shall not murder" ("Thou shalt not kill" in the *KJV*). But does this apply to *all* forms of killing? Should this commandment shape our thinking about self-defense? Or the death penalty? Or abortion? Or war? And, if so, how? Those aren't simple issues, and understanding how God wants us to live out this commandment requires something more than just citing the rule. It requires wisdom.

Luke 2:52 is a verse that absolutely intrigues me. It follows the only story we have about Jesus' boyhood, the incident where he got "lost" in the temple. The verse summarizes Jesus' early years by saying, "And Jesus grew in wisdom and stature, and in favor with God and man." Imagine that! As a boy, as a teenager, as a young man, Jesus himself grew in wisdom. Even Jesus wasn't born with a full measure of wisdom. He acquired it over time. And as he grew in wisdom, he also grew in favor with his heavenly Father.

I believe that's what God desires for each one of us. God wants us to grow in wisdom and favor with him. Theologians sometimes call this process *sanctification*, and God has given us the Wisdom Psalms to assist in that. As we pray the Wisdom Psalms, we become more and more sanctified. God shapes our heart so that we desire and pursue the kind of godly wisdom that enables us to live and walk in ways that honor and please God. God grows in us a heart of wisdom.

Sacred Story Psalms

When Emma and I get ready to go on a walk, I frequently boot up an app on my smartphone called *MapMyWalk*. The app connects to a GPS satellite hundreds of miles away in the sky, locates our precise position, and then traces a map of our route. As we walk, it tells me the distance we've covered, what our pace is, and whatever altitude gain we may have had. I can also pull up a log of our previous walks whenever I wish, and, periodically, the app even sends me an email summarizing our walks. All of that's really pretty cool.

MapMyWalk does a great job of showing me where I've *been* on my walks. However, most of the time you and I go through life looking *ahead*. We're focused on where we're going, not where we've been. We're thinking about the future, not the past. The future's important to be sure, but sometimes it's also good to look back and to remember where we've come from. That's what this app does on a very small scale. It enables me to look back, to the past, and see the paths I've walked. On a much bigger scale, however, several psalms also look back and show us where we've been, where we've come from. These are the Sacred Story Psalms.

To appreciate these psalms, I find it helpful to think of them as *family stories*. These are the stories the ancient Israelites would tell when they got together—not all that different from the way you and I tell family stories when we get together with our siblings and relatives. For instance, my younger sister never fails to remind me that, when we were kids, I would regularly shoot her with rubber bands. I don't remember doing that, but it sounds like something I would've done, so it's probably true. That's a rather silly story, of course, but we also tell more significant ones, such as tales about my mom's parents emigrating from Norway, or my mom and dad meeting on a blind date, or the times our family moved during the years we were growing up. Rehashing old stories like these is one of the reasons we enjoy getting together. Perhaps you can think of a few stories you and your family tell each other.

What is it about family stories? Why do we keep telling them? I think it's because these stories tell us something important about who we are. To see that, imagine for a moment that you were suddenly struck with amnesia and couldn't remember anything about your past. You'd wonder, *Who were my parents, and what were they like? Where did I grow up? Where did I go to school? Who were my childhood friends, and what things did we like to do together?* If we couldn't remember our past, we'd lose a huge part of our identity. We'd no longer know who we are. As Donald Griggs observes, "We know ourselves and are known by others according to the stories we hear, remember, and retell about who we are."[10] So our family stories are a vital part of our identity—even if that includes shooting our sister with rubber bands.

Sacred Story Psalms were one of the ways Israel remembered her corporate story, her story as the family of God's people. There are five psalms that clearly fit into this type: Psalms 78, 105, 106, 135, and 136. It might be

---

10. Griggs, *Psalms – Resource Book*, 41–42.

possible to include the Creation Psalms (Psalms 8, 19, 104, 139, and 148) as a sub-set of Sacred Story Psalms, since they can be seen as stories of how the world came into existence. However, I believe these psalms belong more appropriately in the Praise Psalms category. I'll say more about them in chapter 9 and limit the discussion here to the five more obvious Sacred Story Psalms. Each of these psalms contains a chronological recounting of significant people and events in Israel's history, although the specific people and events vary from psalm to psalm. However, these are not accounts like you'd read in a history book or a travelogue. No, what sets these psalms apart and what makes them *Sacred* Stories is the prominent role that God plays. These are stories of Israel's walk *with God*. God is the One who calls, guides, judges, and rescues his people—over and over again—and we see this in numerous ways throughout these Sacred Story Psalms.

Extra Steps:

Take a few minutes and skim through each of the five Sacred Story Psalms (78, 105, 106, 135, and 136), noticing their similarities and their differences:

>*What events do each of these psalms begin and end with?*

>*What are some of the key events that hold the story together in each psalm?*

>*What actions are attributed to God in these psalms?*

Many psalms broadly refer to God's "works," "acts," "deeds," "wonders," and so forth. Quite often those nouns are enhanced with adjectives like "wonderful," "awesome," "righteous," "great," or "marvelous." In the Sacred Story Psalms, however, the details become more specific and the psalmist recalls *particular* actions and deeds that God had done for his people over the years. For example, Psalm 78 describes in great detail incidents from Israel's time in the wilderness. Psalm 105 names several of Israel's earliest heroes of the faith: Abraham, Isaac, Jacob, and Joseph. Moses and Aaron are also mentioned, as they are in Psalm 106 as well. Out of Israel's many enemies, two are specifically named in both Psalm 135 and Psalm 136: Sihon, the king of the Amorites, and Og, the king of Bashan. Why those two is an interesting but unanswerable question, yet that kind of historical detail is characteristic of Sacred Story Psalms.

Within the Sacred Story Psalms, the most popular "family story" is the Exodus. It appears in all five of these psalms and in at least twelve other psalms as well. No other event figures so prominently in the book of Psalms. God's deliverance of his people out of their slavery in Egypt was as foundational to the Israelites' identity as Jesus' death on the cross is for Christians. It was the proof that God would always remember the covenant he first made with Abraham. We shouldn't be surprised, therefore, to see how often the Exodus is remembered and referred to in the Psalms.

The opening prologue of Psalm 78 (vv. 1–8) provides us with important insight into the purpose for these psalms. So pull out your Bible once again and take a moment to carefully read those first few verses of Psalm 78. As always, I'll wait right here for you.

* * *

So what did you notice? What does the psalmist tell us about how he perceives his reason for recounting this Sacred Story? As I read these opening verses, here's what I see:

I see the psalmist summoning the people to listen to him and to pay attention to his teaching (v. 1), even though he realizes he isn't really telling them anything new. Instead, he's reminding them of "things we have heard and known, things our ancestors have told us" (v. 3). He's looking *back* at "the praiseworthy deeds of the LORD, his power, and the wonders he has done" (v. 4), but he's also looking *forward*. He looks to the past, not simply to relive it or dwell in it, but so the coming generations can be told about those deeds and wonders of the Lord. He believes that he (and the rest of his people) have a sacred responsibility to make sure their children—and "even the children yet to be born" (v. 6)—will know about and never forget all that the Lord has done.

However, the psalmist is not interested in merely passing on information. This isn't like memorizing names and dates in a history class. No, he wants those future generations to know these stories so they won't repeat the errors of their ancestors (v. 8) and so they'll be people who trust in God and keep God's commands (v. 7). The psalmist realizes that these stories of God's ancient dealings with God's people are vital for the people of his day (and for their children) as they move into the future. He's saying, "Go to school on all these people and events that are part of your spiritual heritage."

This theme of remembering the past is also emphasized near the beginning of Psalm 105, another Sacred Story Psalm. The psalmist tells the descendants of Abraham in verse 4, "Remember the wonders he has done, his miracles, and the judgments he pronounced." In Psalm 106, a Sacred Story Psalm that highlights the Israelites' rebellion and disobedience throughout their history, the theme is how the people kept forgetting what the Lord had done:

> "They did *not remember* your many kindnesses" (v. 7).

> "They soon *forgot* what he had done" (v. 13).

> "They *forgot* the God who had saved them" (v. 21).

The ancient Israelites aren't the only ones who need to remember these Sacred Stories, because, you see, these are *our* family stories as well. These are the stories of our spiritual ancestors, and we benefit from remembering them just as much as the psalmists and the people of their day. In fact, remembering their stories does at least three things for us.

First, the Sacred Story Psalms give us *stability* in life. These stories are like deep roots which provide us with confidence both in the present and in the future. Life today is constantly changing, often at breakneck speed. But these psalms remind us that our God is the same yesterday, today, and forever. The God who loved, guided, and rescued his people in ancient days is the same God who loves, guides, and rescues us today.

Second, these psalms give us an *identity*. We become part of a Story that is so much larger than our own individual stories, or even the stories of our individual churches and institutions. We're reminded that we belong to the people of God, to God's family, not just in today's world but throughout all of history. Life today is so individualistic that even our faith often devolves into a simplistic "me and Jesus" formula. Sacred Story Psalms are a valuable counter to that, not by demeaning our own personal story, but by making our story part of something so much bigger, God's Story.

Third, these psalms call us to fulfill a vital *purpose* in life. They give us a Story to tell to our children and to the generation coming after us, so that they too will know and remember—and not forget—all that God has done. That's a call and responsibility we dare not shirk.

As I've been writing this section, I've also been working on memorizing Psalm 105. You might well think this is an odd psalm to memorize—I certainly would have thought so in the past. But I've come to a new appreciation for this psalm and for the other Sacred Story Psalms. As I pray Psalm 105, I remember what God has done for his people in the past, and their story becomes my story. I'm finding that this psalm leads me to praise

God and instills in me a gratitude for belonging to such a powerful, merciful, and loving God. But praying Sacred Story Psalms like Psalm 105 also summons me to renewed confidence, faith, and hope, because God is still writing his Story—with my life as a part of it.

And that's true for your life as well. Our own personal stories did not begin the day we were born. That may be when our biography started, but our sacred story as one of God's children goes back to these ancient stories of these ancient people of God. And, if we look closely enough, we'll see God's work in our lives just as we see it in those Sacred Stories. Running through every part of our story is the hand of God, because our story is a page in God's Story. (Yes, God's Story is a very big book!) Our story, our own personal sacred story, is actually a part of the Great Story that God himself has been working out for all these many years.

Far more of my earthly life is in the past than in the future. Perhaps that's why I find myself becoming a bit more nostalgic, reflecting more on past events and reconnecting with people from earlier periods of my life. Maybe that's just an inevitable aspect of getting older. But maybe that's the Sacred Story Psalms reminding me that there's great value in looking back and remembering where I've come from. As Psalm 105:5 says, "Remember the wonderful works he has done, his miracles, and the judgments he pronounced."

In other words, "Remember the Story!"

Extra Steps:

In Mark 5:1–20 Jesus encounters and heals a demon-possessed man. After his healing, the man begs to go with Jesus. Instead, Jesus tells him, "Go home to your own people and tell them how much the Lord has done for you, and how he has had mercy on you." Based on Jesus' instructions, imagine what this former demoniac's personal Sacred Story Psalm would have been like. What would he have told his family and friends?

Try creating your own Sacred Story Psalm. It probably won't be as dramatic as this man's story, but ask yourself:

Where have I seen God at work in my life?

Over the years, what has God done for me, in me, and through me?

Extra Steps:

At the beginning of this chapter, I gave you a list of eight psalms and asked you to determine what type they are. Here's how I would classify each of them:

Psalm 12 – lament; Psalm 30 – trust or praise; Psalm 42 – lament; Psalm 66 – praise; Psalm 105 – sacred story; Psalm 111 – praise; Psalm 119 – wisdom; and Psalm 121 – trust

Do you disagree with any of these? If so, go back and re-examine those where we differ. Can you see why I might have classified them as I did? Does that change your view of the psalm? Remember: the point is not to determine the "correct" type (after all, even biblical scholars often disagree on this), but to begin to understand the different purposes of the psalms.

Chapter 7

What If It's Dark and Storming?

"My God, my God, why have you forsaken me?
Why are you so far from saving me,
so far from the cries of my anguish?
My God, I cry out by day, but you do not answer,
by night, but I find no rest."

—Psalm 22:1–2

Psalms of Lament

As I write this, Spokane shivers in the frozen grip of winter. The outside temperature gauge reads twelve degrees, the ground is covered with three inches of fresh snow that fell overnight, and the sun has yet to make its appearance, due to the long nights and short days in our northern latitude. All in all, a good day to stay inside.

But regardless of the weather, Emma still needs to go out. So I bundle up, clip the leash on her collar, and out we go for another walk. Emma sniffs at the snow and looks for a place to do her business. She, too, doesn't want to stay out any longer than necessary. In spite of the cold, however, I turn this into another of our holy walks and use the short time we're outside to pray through a couple of psalms—several fewer than if we had the luxury of a longer walk, as we do in the summer or fall. After we come back inside, I dry Emma off, brush the snow from between the pads in her paws, and slowly begin to warm up again.

Even on a wintry morning like this one, I'm thankful I can pray at least a few of the psalms I've learned, psalms that are slowly being written on my heart as I pray them day after day. I pray all types of psalms even on these cold, snowy mornings, but the weather reminds me that there's one type of psalm which is especially appropriate for the dark, stormy, and wintry seasons of life. Not the winters marked by our calendars, but the wintry seasons when life feels like a blizzard, when everything's falling apart, when we're struggling or hurting, and when God seems far away. The psalms truly are prayers for *every* day, and the book of Psalms provides us with prayers that are especially appropriate for those days when it *feels* like a dark and cold winter—even if the temperature gauge reads seventy degrees and the sun's shining brightly in a deep blue sky. These are the Psalms of Lament, and they're the "winter prayers" in the book of Psalms.

Between a third and a half of all the psalms can be considered Psalms of Lament, more than any other single type.[1] Yet, for most of my life as a follower of Jesus, I knew almost nothing about Psalms of Lament. That's because, for the most part, these psalms have been largely ignored in our churches and worship services. They were mentioned in a class I took in seminary, but I don't recall hearing a sermon on a Psalm of Lament until a few years ago, when the Rev. Frank Thomas preached on Psalm 13 during the Calvin Symposium on Worship in January 2012.[2] Shortly after that, I discovered Glenn Pemberton's excellent book, *Hurting with God: Learning To Lament with the Psalms*. My eyes were opened to an entirely new (for me) dimension of prayer.

The Psalms of Lament are not only numerous but they're also quite diverse. Some are subtle, and we might even wonder why they're classified as a Lament. Others are so extreme that we might question why they're included in the Bible at all. Then there are all the other Laments in between. Yet, in spite of all the differences, the Psalms of Lament are marked by five characteristics:

1. The psalmist has a complaint, concern, or question about some situation in life.
2. The psalm is addressed to God, not to the people or to the nations.

---

1. Pemberton classifies sixty of the psalms as Laments (*Hurting with God*, 241). Griggs says that 60-70 psalms can be classified as Laments (*Psalms – Resource Book*, 66).

2. At the time, Rev. Thomas was the pastor of Mississippi Boulevard Christian Church in Memphis, Tennessee. I'm deeply indebted to him for his insightful teaching on this psalm. The Calvin Symposium on Worship is a three-day ecumenical event held each year at Calvin College and Seminary in Grand Rapids, Michigan. For more information, see www.worship.calvin.edu.

3. The psalm is deeply honest, often expressing strong emotions and harsh feelings.
4. The psalmist asks God to do something about the complaint.
5. In spite of everything, the psalmist affirms a confident trust in God.

Not every Psalm of Lament contains all five of these characteristics, but most do. Also, there's no firm order for how they appear in each Lament. That's to be expected, of course, because these prayers are not following a template; they're expressing the heart of the psalmist. Still, they do generally share in these five characteristics.

To unpack these characteristics, turn in your Bible to Psalm 13, the Lament that introduced me to this important type of psalm. Take a few moments to read through this short psalm three or four times. Read it slowly and allow yourself to feel the emotions of the psalmist. Can you identify with any of those feelings?

Go ahead and read it. And take your time.

* * *

So, what did you notice? One of the first things most people notice is the series of four questions that begins the psalm. Four times the psalmist asks the question, "How long?" With each repetition we can sense his growing frustration and despair. Clearly, he's in the midst of some very difficult life situation. Here are three issues the psalmist is struggling with:

1. The psalm is attributed to David (and there's no reason to believe he didn't write it), and David certainly had many *enemies*. Perhaps he was being threatened by one of them, or maybe his political foes were on the verge of defeating him. "How long will my enemy triumph over me?" he asks.

2. Some commentators suggest that David was quite ill when he prayed this prayer. I'm not so sure about that, but he was obviously *depressed*: "How long must I wrestle with my thoughts and day after day have sorrow in my heart?" If you've ever struggled with depression, you can relate to what David was feeling.

3. Probably the most poignant complaint in the psalm, however, is *God's silence*, God's apparent absence. David begins his prayer by telling God that he feels forgotten and abandoned by God: "How long, Lord? Will you forget me forever? How long will you hide your face from

me?" Perhaps you've heard the expression, "If God seems distant, guess who moved?" Well, David would not have bought into that bit of pop theology. No, he felt like God was far away—but *David* wasn't the one who had moved. Rather, God was hiding his face from David, a situation that was causing David great anguish.

David's frustration with God seems to rise to the level of genuine anger. In verses 3 and 4 David sounds much like an angry parent who's trying to get the attention of a misbehaving child. In such a situation, the parent might bark, "Look at me when I'm talking to you!" That's the way David sounds when he says, "Look on me and answer, Lord my God." He's angry, but he's also desperate: "Give light to my eyes or I will sleep in death." *God, you have to do something, or I'm going to die!*

C. S. Lewis once went through a tough spiritual struggle that seems remarkably similar to the one David was going through when he wrote Psalm 13. When Lewis was in his fifties, he married a woman named Joy Gresham. She was the love of his life, and they were incredibly happy together. But after just four years of marriage, Joy came down with cancer and died. Lewis wrote a book about his time of grieving entitled *A Grief Observed*. In the book Lewis expresses many of the strong doubts that he wrestled with, such as this:

> Meanwhile, where is God? . . . When you are happy, . . . if you . . . turn to Him with gratitude and praise, you will be—or so it feels—welcomed with open arms. But go to Him when your need is desperate, when all other help is vain, and what do you find? A door slammed in your face, and a sound of bolting and double bolting on the inside. After that, silence.[3]

Lewis didn't doubt God's existence; that wasn't the issue. No, the problem came for Lewis precisely because he *did* believe that God existed, but God seemed blind and deaf to his pain. I think he could have related very well to David's questioning of God in Psalm 13, to the anger and the hurt.

Lewis's and David's spiritual struggles are but two examples of the kinds of complaints, problems, and crises that inspired the numerous Psalms of Lament. Many of those complaints and crises involved enemies of some kind—so much so that Eugene Peterson can state, "The Psalms are full of unsettling enemy talk. God is the primary subject in the Psalms, but

---

3. Lewis, *A Grief Observed*, 4.

enemies are established in solid second place."[4] Indeed, among the Psalms of Lament, only a handful don't refer to enemies of some kind.

Who are these enemies, and what are we to make of them for our own prayers? They aren't simply people who disagree with us or who've insulted us or hurt us in some way. No, the enemies in the Psalms of Lament are reflections of the evil that pollutes our world. As Pemberton says, "The enemy is anyone or even anything that stands against life, the community, or against God and God's way in the world."[5]

Even a cursory glance at a newspaper or a social media feed illustrates the breadth of evil and wickedness in our world. Again and again, we observe evil people doing much harm to other people and to the world—and sometimes to ourselves, our friends, and our loved ones. The Laments are prayers that tackle such evil head on. Most often these enemies in the psalms are unnamed and ambiguous, like in Psalm 13, which allows us to more easily substitute our own enemies into the psalmists' prayers. Our enemies might be real people. Or the enemies might be diseases or natural disasters. Or they might be the devil and his minions (1 Peter 5:8).

So, when I pray the Psalms and pray about enemies, I, too, am confronting the evil in our world. Even if the enemies are not my own, I can be praying for a friend or family member who is wrestling with an enemy of some kind. Or I can be praying for Christian brothers and sisters around the world who are facing the forces of evil. As I pray about enemies in the Psalms of Lament, I'm bringing the world's evils before the only One who can truly do something about them.

Of course, enemies aren't the only reason for the psalmists' laments. In fact, virtually any negative life experience we can imagine has a parallel in one of the Psalms of Lament. For instance, Psalm 6:2 refers to some kind of physical sickness; Psalm 31:9–10 mentions grief; Psalm 51:2–5 references the psalmist's personal sin; Psalm 60:1 has the background of a military defeat; Psalm 74:3–4 bemoans the destruction of the temple; Psalm 94:2–7 lists the woes of oppression; and Psalm 109:25 describes the helplessness caused by false accusers. The scope of issues in the Laments seems almost limitless.

---

4. Peterson, *Answering God*, 95.
5. Pemberton, *Hurting with God*, 121.

Extra Steps:

To explore the variety of concerns in the Laments, read through Psalms 7, 10, 12, 41, 43, 55, and 56. As you read each psalm, ask yourself:

> What is the psalmist's lament (complaint, problem, situation)?

> What does he want God to do?

An image that captures many of these hard situations is "the pit," which occurs sixteen times in the Psalms. Typical examples include: "You spared me from going down to the pit" (Psalm 30:3); "You have put me in the lowest pit, in the darkest depths" (Psalm 88:6); "Who redeems your life from the pit" (Psalm 103:4); and "Do not hide your face from me or I will be like those who go down to the pit" (Psalm 143:7). It's an ancient image that still has a powerful impact in our modern world.

In its literal sense, a pit was a cistern or a well. Pits were often muddy with slimy walls, making escape impossible without assistance. We see this, for instance, in Genesis 37:21–28 where Joseph's brothers placed him in a pit as a kind of holding cell. Jeremiah also was put into a pit by some of his enemies, a place where he was expected to die from exposure and starvation (Jer. 38:6–9).

Walter Brueggemann deduces from this that the pit was a place where a person was essentially removed from life (even if they remained alive). In the pit, they were cut off from their family and friends, and they lacked any power or control over their life. He notes that "the pit" can thus refer metaphorically to the experience of being powerless or forgotten or abandoned, characteristics of severe depression.[6]

In the colloquial language of our day, we might call this experience "the pits." It's a condition in life that anyone would certainly hope to avoid, and thus the psalmists' earnest prayers for God to prevent them from going down to the pit (or into the pits). And when they've been in the pit (or the pits) and God has brought them out, they eagerly join in giving God their grateful praise. Those are prayers many of us can understand all too well.

Life situations caused by our enemies or by the pit/pits also produce plenty of raw emotion, like we see in Psalm 13. Fear, despair, anger, frustration, hatred, desperation, doubt, violence, and longing for vengeance and

---

6. Brueggemann, *Praying the Psalms*, 32–37.

vindication—you'll find them all in the Psalms of Lament. Sometimes those intense emotional expressions can be hard to hear, especially for Christians. At best, they seem inappropriate; at worst, they seem un-Christian. After all, didn't Jesus tell us to love our enemies and pray for our persecutors (Matt. 5:44 and Luke 6:27–28)? Didn't the Apostle Paul tell us that "in all things God works for the good of those who love him" (Rom. 8:28)? And that we should "rejoice in the Lord always" (Phil. 4:4) and "give thanks in all circumstances" (1 Thess. 5:18)? Didn't the Apostle James say we should face trials with "pure joy" (Jas. 1:2)?

The obvious answer is, yes, they did say all those things. Jesus, Paul, and James tell us what we *should* feel about our enemies and about the problems and crises of life. They tell us what we ought to aspire towards. But I suspect most of us are not quite there yet—at least not when the punch in the gut hits us hard enough. We live in a broken, fallen world where evil sometimes wins battles, where wicked people sometimes do awful things, and where tragedies sometimes strike even the best people. So what do we do then? What do we do when we *do* hate that person who has harmed us? Or when we *do* feel like we've gotten a raw deal, or that someone's taken advantage of us? Or when God seems deaf to our pleas? What do we do with the various emotions we inevitably feel in such situations?

One option is to bury our feelings. *Don't let them see you cry!* Just hold them in, ignore them, pretend they aren't really there. *Don't worry, be happy!* Of course, the problem with this response is that it often leads to depression, or ulcers, or even "going postal." Burying our emotions is no solution.

Another way to deal with our negative emotions is to hold a "pity party." Get together with another person or with a group of friends and complain to each other. *Misery loves company!* Now everyone can be miserable, and, of course, nothing about the situation has changed.

A third way we wrongly handle our negative emotions is when we take them out on others. *Let 'em know how you really feel!* However, a lot of relationships get wrecked when people do this. Angry words can't be taken back, and many actions are tough to undo. Taken to the extreme, spousal abuse and child abuse can also occur when we direct our negative feelings towards the ones we love.

But the Psalms of Lament show us another way—God's way. I've said that the book of Psalms—God's Prayer Book—is intended to teach us how to pray. If that's the case, then we can say that the Psalms of Lament are intended to teach us how to pray when we're in great pain, or when life feels like it's falling apart, or when we're utterly desperate, or when our prayers are not being answered. They're the God-given responses to the suffering, injustice, and sin that we experience in life. The title of Glenn Pemberton's book on the Laments captures this purpose very well: *Hurting with God*. The Psalms of Lament are, as Pemberton puts it, "a way to 'hurt with God' when we are in the middle of a storm."[7]

The dictionary defines a "lament" as an expression of grief or sorrow. This means that laments are not necessarily prayers. One can lament all kinds of things in life without that lament becoming a prayer. One can express deep sorrow, regret, doubt, or anger without ever bringing those feelings before God. To lament is not necessarily to pray.

But the Psalms of Lament are first of all prayers before they are anything else. As we've seen in Psalm 13, David wrestles *with God* about God's silence and apparent absence. He questions God. He can't understand why God isn't answering him. Nevertheless, David still addresses his complaint *to God*. He isn't crafting his words for the benefit of other people. He isn't seeking the wisdom of another person. He isn't griping to his friends. No, David is *praying*. His words are addressed to God. He is hurting *with God*.

As Bonhoeffer writes, "There is in the Psalms no quick and easy resignation to suffering. There is always struggle, anxiety, doubt. . . . But even in the deepest hopelessness God alone remains the one addressed."[8] In the Psalms of Lament, God invites you and me to bring our deepest hurts, our darkest feelings, our most profound doubts to him. And so the Psalms of Lament become our prayers.

Praying with Brutal Honesty

The Psalms of Lament, then, are first of all prayers, but even more than that, they're *honest* prayers. These are not sanitized prayers or churchy prayers. They aren't polite prayers or nice prayers. What they are is frank and direct and real.

---

7. Pemberton, *Hurting with God*, 75. The phrase "hurt with God" actually came from an essay that a student wrote for one of Pemberton's classes. The student wrote how praying Psalm 13 had enabled him to "hurt with God" as he coped with a very hard period of his college life.

8. Bonhoeffer, *Psalms*, 47.

The so-called *Imprecatory Psalms* show us just how brutally honest the psalmists' prayers could be. The word "imprecate" means to invoke a curse, and these psalms are ones that ask God to judge, shame, or destroy the enemies of the psalmist. Frequently, these imprecatory requests are brief, almost passing, pleas, but in at least eight psalms (35, 58, 59, 69, 79, 83, 109, and 137) they become even more violent and vindictive in their hatred for the enemies. Two of the most shocking examples are in Psalm 109:6–15 ("May his days be few; . . . may his children be fatherless and his wife a widow") and Psalm 137:8–9 ("Happy is the one who seizes your infants and dashes them against the rocks"). Perhaps one of the more creative curses is "May they be like a slug that melts away as it moves along" (Psalm 58:8).

Many Christians (including C. S. Lewis) believe these are sub-Christian prayers which we should effectively excise from our Bibles in light of the teachings of the New Testament. But if we're offended by the language and emotions in these psalms, we need to remember that God himself chose to include them in our Bibles. If we truly believe that "all Scripture is God-breathed and is useful for teaching, rebuking, correcting and training in righteousness" (2 Tim. 3:16), then we must conclude that this also includes the Imprecatory Psalms. But if God placed these psalms in his Prayer Book, what is he trying to teach us through them?

Could it be that the Imprecatory Psalms illustrate just how much honesty God desires in our prayers? Admittedly, these are some of the most difficult psalms in God's Prayer Book, but we must realize that these curses are requests for *God* to judge or condemn the enemies; the psalmists aren't taking vengeance into their own hands. Reflecting on these psalms, Philip Yancey points out, "We readers are 'overhearing' prayers addressed to God. Seen in this way, the cursing psalms are what I have called 'spiritual therapy' taken to its limits."[9] He describes them as "primal-scream prayers," screams that, in the midst of life's worst experiences, resound in the psalmist's soul and make their way to God as prayers.

When we view the Imprecatory Psalms in that way, we understand that they express how the psalmists truly felt at the time, even though they aren't saying that you or I should feel the same way. However, since God didn't censor these from his Prayer Book, they do show us the value God places on complete honesty in prayer. These psalms teach us that God wants us to bring all of our emotions to him, no matter how awful they might seem. God

---

9. Yancey, Philip. "How I Learned to Stop Hating and Start Loving the Psalms." *Christianity Today* (Oct. 6, 1989) 30.

doesn't want us cleaning up our prayers, or telling him what we think he wants to hear from us. God wants us to tell him what we're really feeling and thinking. God wants honest prayers, even brutally honest prayers.[10]

This means that nothing is inappropriate or out of bounds in our prayers as long as we're expressing the true feelings and thoughts that reside in our heart. As Jim Sire writes in the conclusion to his book, *Learning To Pray Through the Psalms*, "Honest prayer—is there any other kind?—comes from the depths of our heart. There is no question of fooling God. We cannot sneak up on him with silvery tongue, sing his praises, and at the same time harbor resentment of either him or others."[11]

David, the author of Psalm 23 with all its blissfulness and delight, was also the author of Psalm 13 with all its anger and frustration. And Jesus himself, feeling the pain of separation from his heavenly Father, made the words of a Psalm of Lament his prayer from the cross: "My God, my God, why have you forsaken me?" (Mark 15:34, quoting from Psalm 22:1). As you and I learn to pray the Psalms of Lament, we follow their example. In the Psalms of Lament, we bring even our ugliest thoughts, our worst desires, and our strongest feelings to God. Instead of burying those emotions or taking them out on others, we bring them to God.

Praying into Grace

So the Psalms of Lament are rooted in complaints (laments) about something in life, but they're prayers because they're addressed to God and because they're brutally honest and real. However, the Psalms of Lament are not just a God-given means for us to vent about life's problems. God isn't just giving us a way to get things off our chest. God has a much deeper purpose in mind, and to see that we need to go back once again to Psalm 13. There's a great mystery in this psalm, and I wonder if you saw it when you read through the psalm earlier. Before I go on to explain the mystery, perhaps you'd like to go back and read the psalm once more.

* * *

The mystery is this: How do we get from verse 4 to verse 5? There's a chasm between those two verses in Psalm 13 that's wider than the Grand Canyon.

10. For more discussion on Imprecatory Psalms, see Pemberton, *Hurting with God*, 133-46, and Yancey, *The Bible Jesus Read*, 133-9.

11. Sire, *Learning To Pray*, 214.

The little word "But" at the beginning of verse 5 is like when you're riding on a roller coaster, zooming along in one direction, and suddenly the roller coaster changes directions, and the gravitational forces whip you around and pin you back in your seat. After reading David's questions and complaints in verses 1–4, verse 5 comes at us so unexpectedly that we almost have to go back and see if we skipped a few verses. What did we overlook? Did we miss some fine print between verse 4 and verse 5?

There are no easy answers to this mystery. No simple formulas. I can't do what Job's friends did and tell you to find some hidden sin in your life, confess it, and everything will be okay. Life doesn't work that way. But I can tell you that you don't get to verse 5 unless you first pray verses 1–4. Somehow the prayer of verses 1–4 leads to the prayer of verses 5–6.

Ann Weems is a Christian author who lost her son under tragic circumstances.[12] He was just twenty-one years old at the time, and Ann was utterly devastated by his death. Her friends did everything they could to help her, of course, but the grief seemed to be more than she could bear. Then one day someone suggested she express her mourning by writing her own psalms of lament, since she was, after all, a writer. So Ann began doing that. She wrote prayers where she poured out her pain and asked deep questions. For instance, here's one prayer that she wrote:

> O God, what am I going to do? He's gone, and I'm left. With an empty pit in my life. . . . How could You have allowed this to happen? I thought You protected Your own! You are the power. Why didn't You use it? You are the glory. But there was no glory in his death. You are justice and mercy. Yet there was no justice, no mercy for him.

Sounds a little like Psalm 13, doesn't it? Ann Weems began her prayer of lament like Psalm 13, angry with God and questioning God's lack of action. But she also concluded her prayer like Psalm 13. Here's where she ended up:

> O Holy One, I am confident that You will save me. . . . You are the power and the glory. You are justice and mercy. You are my God forever.

We don't always go so quickly from verse 4 to verse 5. In fact, I wonder how quickly David did? What kind of time gap do you suppose there

---

12. This story is recounted in a sermon by H. Mark Abbott entitled "Lent: Learning to Lament Psalm 13," downloaded from www.preaching.com on Feb. 27, 2012.

was between verse 4 and verse 5 for David? Do you suppose David prayed verses 1–4 over and over, day after day, for a long time, before he was finally able to pray verses 5–6? I think he may well have.

But the point is that when we begin praying verses 1–4, when we begin crying out to God with our laments, with our questions, and even with our anger, we open our heart to God's grace. Our prayers are always a response to God's grace. No prayer has ever been uttered that wasn't preceded in some way by God's grace. And so when we cry to God in our anguish and anger—in our laments—we're actually responding to God's grace. But in the process we're also opening our heart to God and allowing God's grace to mysteriously work in our heart.

Here's a truth we often forget: Prayer is not intended to make us feel better about life; prayer is intended to draw us closer to God. We won't pray a prayer of lament if we don't care about God. When we *do* care about God, when we do love God, that's when we pray the way David does here in Psalm 13. A prayer of lament doesn't show a lack of faith. It actually shows a deep faith and trust, a deep relationship with God. And through prayers of lament we grow even closer to God. It may take some time, but eventually God's grace enables us to say, as David did in verses 5–6, "But I trust in your unfailing love. My heart rejoices in your salvation. I will sing the Lord's praise, for he has been good to me."

Some years ago I resigned as the pastor of the church I was serving, because I sensed the Lord telling me it was time for a change—both for me and for the church. At the time, I was confident I would find another position before too long. After all, wasn't I doing what I thought God wanted me to do? Wasn't I following God's leading? But as the months went by and nothing came along, the doubts multiplied. And so did the questions: *Why did God lead me down this dead end path?* Then the anger: *Where is God anyway? Doesn't God care?* I felt like a player on the end of the bench, a player who never gets into the game and who wonders if the coach even remembers his name. I thought I had the abilities to help the team, so why did it seem like the coach had forgotten all about me?

During this time, I continued to worship in various churches, although I'm not sure I was actually worshiping. My body was there in the sanctuary, but my heart was often somewhere else. The worship teams led us in all kinds of praise songs, but I rarely sang. It was just too hard.

After two years "on the bench" I finally got back in the "game." God opened the doors for me to work part-time at two churches, and I began to sense God's presence and blessing once again. Slowly, the dark night of my soul began to brighten with the light of dawn. And part of that healing process has been learning to pray the Psalms, which came about through my new ministry at those two churches.

As I've looked back on that very difficult period in my life, I've wondered: *Would it have been different if I'd known about the Psalms of Lament?* Mostly, I stopped talking to God when I no longer felt God's presence or love. But what if I had been familiar with Psalm 13 back then? What if I could have taken various Psalms of Lament and made them my prayers? If I had been able to do that, I believe I would have experienced God's grace much more fully and much more quickly than I did. And that's why I'm sharing that dark period in my life with you. My hope is that you will find God's grace by praying the Psalms of Lament when you go through the hard times of life.

Psalms of Lament may be winter prayers, but winter eventually gives way to spring. Winter may leave its marks behind, its damage, but with the spring comes new life. These psalms teach us that the way through the hurts, the struggles, and the questions we experience lies in bringing all of our emotions, feelings, and doubts to the God who loves us more than we can ever know. As we pray our brutally honest laments, God's grace does its work in our soul. God gives us the grace to trust that he'll be with us no matter whether our prayers are answered or not. We begin to find peace. God gives us the strength we need. We feel God's love once again. And God's grace enables us to say, "My world's a mess right now, but I know I belong to God, and I know that God is good."

So, are you going through a wintry season in life right now? Are you in the midst of a blizzard or a storm? Are you hurting in some way? Do you feel like God is absent from your life? Are you angry with God because of something that happened in your life? If so, maybe it's time to start praying some Psalms of Lament. Maybe it's time to let God's grace go to work in your heart and enable you to move from verse 4 to verse 5.

Extra Steps:

Carefully read through Psalm 143. Then compare this psalm with the five characteristics of a Psalm of Lament which were listed near the beginning of this chapter.

What is the psalmist's lament and how does he want God to deliver him?

Are there any parts of this psalm that you can especially identify with? If so, read through the psalm again (out loud, if possible), this time making it your prayer to God.

Chapter 8

The Journey's Destination

"I will exalt you, my God the King;
 I will praise your name for ever and ever.
Every day I will praise you
 and extol your name for ever and ever."

—Psalm 145:1–2

Psalms of Praise

The sun is out this morning, and I've decided to take Emma for a walk in the state park a couple of miles from our home. When she figures out that we're going for a walk *and* a ride—well, her whole body shakes with her excitement. For Emma, car rides are at the top of her list of fun things to do in life. (Except for eating, of course.) So, as soon as I open the car door, she hops in, and we drive off.

The parking area is on top of a bluff, and we hike down a woodsy, switchback trail. The Little Spokane River meanders through here, and another trail leads us through a field and to a small footbridge that crosses the river. It's a spectacular morning, and Emma and I have the area all to ourselves. The early-morning sunlight makes the autumn leaves even more colorful. I can hear the river, but only if I stop and listen carefully. Mostly, it's just quiet and peaceful.

Looking around, I spot four deer a short distance away in the field. They stare back but don't seem overly concerned. Emma doesn't even notice them. She just keeps sniffing around the path while I stop and watch the deer. Such beautiful creatures, I think to myself.

Just then, a large hawk swoops through the air above us and perches on top of a tree nearby. It may simply be searching for its next meal, but I find myself envying the hawk for getting to see such views every day.

As I attempt to take in the entire scene, I'm overcome with the wonder of the moment. *Wow, God! What an incredible Creator you are! Thank you for allowing me to share in this!* Words come to my lips from one of the psalms I've been heart-learning: "How many are your works, LORD! In wisdom you made them all; the earth is full of your creatures" (Psalm 104:24).

Walking along the river, enjoying the fall colors, seeing the deer and the hawk—it was one of those "Wow!" moments when I couldn't help but offer my praise to the God who had created all this and who had so wonderfully orchestrated that morning's holy walk.

Extra Steps:

Recall a "Wow!" experience that you've had, and relive the experience in your mind or describe it to a friend. What was it about the experience that made such an impact on you?

How did you respond to your "Wow!" experience at the time? Do you see it any differently as you look back on it now?

In the previous chapter, I said that Psalms of Lament are prayers for the winters of life and that they provide us with the words to voice our questions, worries, and fears in prayers to God. In contrast, Psalms of Praise are especially befitting those "Wow, God!" moments in life, as well as those times when we feel especially grateful or loving towards God. In short, they provide us with the words and prayers to express our wonder, gratitude, and love to God. In this chapter, I'm going to examine these psalms and discuss what's really happening when we offer our praises to God.

It's no surprise, of course, that the book of Psalms contains Psalms of Praise. (Actually, I suspect most people are likely to be surprised at how many of the psalms are *not* Psalms of Praise.) I've already noted that the Hebrew title of the book is *Tehillim*, which means "Praises" (see chapter 5). In addition, there are at least 138 verses in the Psalms that include some form of the word "praise," and the idea of praising God is included in most of the psalms, including Psalms of Trust, Wisdom Psalms, Sacred Story Psalms, and even the Psalms of Lament.

THE JOURNEY'S DESTINATION

So, obviously, praising God is a major theme in God's Prayer Book. Nevertheless, only about thirty psalms should strictly be classified as Psalms of Praise. These are Psalms 8, 29, 30, 33, 47, 48, 65, 72, 84, 92, 93, 95, 100, 103, 104, 111, 113, 114, 117, 118, 124, 135, 136, 138, and 145–150. Praise and gratitude to God is the central purpose for each of these psalms.

In categorizing these psalms, I should note three clarifications. First, remember that if a psalm can be categorized as one of the other types of psalms (Trust, Wisdom, Sacred Story, or Lament), that's where I prefer to place it, even if it does contain elements of praise (as most of the psalms do). The key lies in the *overall purpose* of each particular psalm.

Second, I include psalms here that others would categorize separately as *Psalms of Thanksgiving*. While many people attempt to distinguish between praise for who God is and thanksgiving for what God has done, I find that's often a difficult distinction to maintain in practice. Look, for example, at Psalm 100 which uses "thanksgiving" and "praise" as virtual synonyms, or Psalm 52:9, which says, "For what you have done I will always praise you." So I prefer to see gratitude as a form of praise and to view Psalms of Thanksgiving as simply a variation among the Psalms of Praise.[1]

Third, I've also included several psalms that others might label instead as *Royal Psalms* or *Songs of Zion*. While I appreciate the reasons for labeling those psalms as separate types, I prefer to simplify the typology by placing them in other categories, usually as either Psalms of Praise or Psalms of Trust. Classifications such as "Royal Psalm" or "Song of Zion" are based on how scholars believe those psalms were originally used by the ancient Israelites. While I don't dispute such historical usage, I'm more interested in how God's people are to use the psalms *today*. The contemporary relevance of Royal Psalms and Songs of Zion is more apparent when we view them as Praise Psalms or Psalms of Trust (or even perhaps as Sacred Story Psalms).

With those clarifications in mind, the differences between a Psalm of Praise and all those other psalms that contain praise becomes more clear. As I've already noted, the primary distinguishing characteristic is that the *central purpose* of these psalms is praise (or gratitude) to God. However, Psalms of Praise generally include several other common elements as well:

---

1. Timothy Keller takes this same view about praise and thanksgiving. See the discussion of this in his book, *Prayer*, 195. Chapter 12 in that book ("Awe: Praising His Glory") is an insightful exploration of the importance and role of praise in our prayers.

- Praise Psalms usually contain direct statements about the psalmist's intention to praise God, often using various synonyms for "praise," such as "bless," "exalt," "honor," "glorify," or "extol."

- In many Praise Psalms a past distress is recalled, along with God's deliverance from the distress. This is especially characteristic of Psalms of Thanksgiving. See, for example, Psalm 30, where the psalmist praises (and thanks) God for having healed him from some life-threatening illness or injury. Notice that the difference between these psalms and a Psalm of Lament is that in Praise Psalms the distress is in the past, while in a Lament the psalmist is still experiencing the distress.

- The Praise Psalms often speak in a more generic sense of God's "wonders," "acts," "deeds," and so forth. However, since these are *God's* actions, adjectives like "awesome," "mighty," or "powerful" are frequently added to the nouns to set them apart from more ordinary acts and deeds. Traits of God such as mercy, compassion, and love are said to be seen in the ways God acts on behalf of his people, and those provide additional motivation for praising God.

- Praise Psalms frequently call for others to join the psalmist in praising God. The desire to praise God is simply too great for the psalmist to keep it to himself.

So those are several characteristics of Psalms of Praise, but let's move away from generalities and consider an actual example.

A Masterpiece of Praise to God

We could examine any of a number of Psalms of Praise to learn more about this type of psalm. However, one of my personal favorites is Psalm 145. As you may recall from chapter 1, my journey into God's Prayer Book began with this psalm. Take a few minutes and read through it, noticing the tremendous variety of praises that are offered to God. Go ahead and start reading. As usual, I'll wait right here for you . . . .

Extra Steps:

As you notice the various things for which David praises God in Psalm 145, which ones are especially meaningful to you right now, and why? Take a moment to thank God for those things.

Psalm 145 is the last psalm attributed to David, and it's a magnificent, personal declaration of praise to God. I pointed out at the end of chapter 5 that it's an acrostic psalm in which each verse begins with a different Hebrew letter, in order through the entire alphabet. Although we can't be sure of the purpose for writing a psalm as an acrostic, it certainly represents a lot of careful work and deep thought. So Psalm 145 wasn't just a spontaneous outburst of praise on David's part. It was well thought out and carefully constructed. Perhaps this explains why devout Jews would recite this psalm three times a day in their synagogues. They recognized it as a masterpiece of praise to God.

Like many Psalms of Praise, this one begins with the author's personal commitment to praise God. In verses 1 and 2 David declares, "I will exalt you," "I will praise your name," and "Every day I will praise you." He concludes the psalm in a similar manner in verse 21: "My mouth will speak in praise of the LORD." His final words invite "every creature" to join him in praising God "for ever and ever." These opening and closing declarations indicate David's purpose for writing the psalm. Combined with the acrostic format, it's clear that David was going all out to praise God in this psalm.

Between these bookend commitments to praise God, David runs through a broad listing of God's attributes and actions (vv. 3–20). Together, all these attributes and actions reflect God's "name," which David refers to in the opening two verses and again in the very last verse. For Jews, a person's name was much more than just an identifying label. A person's name conveyed their character and their personality. It told you something about who they *are*. So when David refers to praising God's "name," that's shorthand for God's character and for all that God does because of who God is—some of which David spells out in the body of the psalm.

When we praise another person, it usually means we've identified something about the person that we admire and appreciate. We've noticed something they've done or some character quality in them that we want to lift up so that others will also recognize what we see in that person. That's what David's doing here by praising God's "name." He's lifting up God's character, God's nature, and God's attributes, along with God's actions and deeds—all those qualities that make David go *Wow!* as he contemplates them. He's lifting all that up so that everyone can see all those things and admire them along with him. This is why David uses "exalt" and "extol" as synonyms for "praise" here in the first couple of verses. "Exalt" stresses this idea of lifting up, and "extol" emphasizes a kind of public declaration.

From this, allow me to pose a simple definition: *To praise God is to recognize, admire, and verbalize both who God is and what God has done.* In other words, praising God is a way that we get specific in our admiration and worship of God. We tell God (and anyone else who's listening) what we admire and appreciate about him. We hold up those qualities and actions that have caused us to give our lives over to God and bow before him in worship.

Throughout this psalm we see various ways in which David does that. For instance, in verse 4 David talks about one generation "commending" God's works to another. In other places he talks about "telling" or "speaking" or "proclaiming." He also mentions "celebrating" and "meditating" and "singing." This shows that we can praise God in all kinds of ways. But whatever form our expressions of praise take, the central idea is that we're recognizing, admiring, and verbalizing who God is and what God has done.

Extra Steps:

Do you agree or disagree with my definition of praising God? How might you improve on it?

Read through one or two other Praise Psalms (29, 33, 65, 84, 103, 111, and 135 would be especially good to choose from). Compare the style of praising God in those psalms with what we've seen in Psalm 145. How are they similar? How are they different?

Praising God: What Are We Really Doing?

As we reflect on the Psalms of Praise and the place of praising God in the book of Psalms, we should back up a bit and consider more deeply what praising God is really all about. "Recognizing, admiring, and verbalizing who God is and what God has done" may be a good description of the act of praising God, but there are deeper issues we need to wrestle with. For example, why do we praise God in the first place? And what are we really doing when we praise God?

We need to ask these questions because it's easy to misunderstand why we praise God. When we praise a person for something, we may do so with all kinds of motivations. As I suggested above, it may be that we've noticed something about the person that we admire and appreciate and want to hold up so that others can join us in our admiration. But on other occasions, we may think the person wants or expects to hear praise from us, like when we shake the pastor's hand after a worship service and say, "Good sermon, Pastor!" We may also hope that our praise will cause the person to think more highly of us and then do something for us as a result: "Great job on that presentation, Boss! Uh, do you think I can have Friday off?" Or we may offer our praise hoping it will encourage or build the person up in some way and help them to do better. It's all too easy to view the act of praising God as being similar to affirming, flattering, or buttering up another person, even if we wouldn't perhaps express it in quite those words. We might not even realize that's what we're doing.

In his book, *Reflections on the Psalms*, C. S. Lewis explains how praising God was actually a stumbling block on his pathway to faith in God. He had a difficult time with religious people who made it sound as though we have a duty to praise God or, even worse, who said that God demands our praise. These views about praising God caused Lewis to envision God as being like a person who constantly needs to be assured of how good, smart, or charming they are—hardly someone we'd be drawn to, much less desire to worship. Lewis writes that he could understand gratitude, reverence, and obedience to God but not a "perpetual eulogy."[2]

While I've never felt quite like Lewis on this issue, I have found myself wondering what I'm really doing when I praise God. Perhaps you have as well. Am I somehow stroking God's divine ego, if God could even be said to have such a thing? Ego-stroking is certainly behind some of the "praise" we give to other people: "Susie, you played such a wonderful game! Yes, you struck out three times, but you looked so good doing it!" However, Lewis is right in criticizing the notion of a God who would need to have ego-stroking of any kind. There simply can be no sense in which God *needs* my praise.

But if I'm not trying to make God feel better about himself by praising him, am I somehow attempting to butter God up so that he'll love me more, feel better about me, or grant me something I'm asking him for? When we actually put it like that, however, it's obvious how ludicrous such a view is. Would God ever love me, or you, or anyone else, any less because we didn't praise him enough? Of course not.

But then what *are* we doing when we praise God?

---

2. Lewis, *Reflections*, 90–98.

Lewis' view about praising God changed when he realized that anytime we enjoy something, our joy naturally wants to express itself in praise. When we delight in *anything*—a song that grabs us, a great athletic performance, a good book, a delicious meal, a heart-warming story, whatever—our natural response is to praise the object of our joy. Praise is simply a natural outcome and fulfillment of that joy, and without the praise, our joy would be incomplete and lessened.

In addition, Lewis noticed that our own praise rarely seems adequate. We also want others to share that joy by joining in praise with us. And, of course, the greater the object of our joy, the greater our praise and the more we want others to share in it. Lewis concluded that, in calling everyone to praise God, the psalmists were simply doing what all people do when they speak about something they care deeply about.[3]

That's certainly what I was doing on the holy walk I described at the beginning of this chapter. I wasn't praising God because I thought it was my duty or because I thought God might appreciate my words of gratitude. Nor was I attempting to ingratiate myself with God. No, I was praising God because that was the *only* way I could respond to four deer, a swooping hawk, and a beautiful day.

Praise Psalms are for moments like that, for those times when we can't help but go, "Wow, God!"[4] A beautiful sunset takes our breath away. Or we're overwhelmed with a sense of God's forgiveness. Or the starry sky reminds us how immense the universe is. Or something utterly amazing happens, something completely unexplainable but also completely good. Or we simply have a deep sense of peace, of *shalôm*.

What do we say on such occasions? So often our own words seem so inadequate, but Praise Psalms give us the words to respond. In their various ways, they enable us to respond, "Wow, God!" We make them our prayers, not because God needs our praise or because we're trying to manipulate God in some way, but because the situation, the moment, the experience opens our eyes to God, and praise is the only way we *can* respond. *Wow, God!*

But Praise Psalms are not just for those "Wow, God!" moments. Often our joy in God is sparked by something particular that God has done for us,

---

3. Lewis, *Reflections*, 95.

4. Anne Lamott has written a short but rather profound book on prayer entitled, *Help, Thanks, Wow: The Three Essential Prayers*. Her third essential prayer, Wow, provides some helpful perspective on the nature of Praise Psalms. I'm indebted to her for the characterization of Praise Psalms as ways to express our sense of *Wow! or Thanks!*

perhaps an answer to a prayer or some unexpected gift or blessing. When we realize the gift or blessing has come from the gracious hand of God himself, we naturally want to respond with gratitude. We want to say, "Thanks, God!" and many of the Praise Psalms help us do precisely that. They show the psalmists pouring out their thankfulness to God, and as we pray these psalms, they become our expressions of gratitude to God as well. However, our gratitude quickly turns into praise for God himself, not just for what God has given us. Our joy is not simply in the gift we've received but even more so in the Giver of the gift. *Thanks, God!*

In addition to saying, "Wow, God!" or "Thanks, God!" the Psalms of Praise also give us a way to say simply, "I love you, God!" Through Praise Psalms, we're able to tell God how much we love him because of who he is and what he's done. Someone has said that "praise is the language of lovers," and that's certainly true in the Psalms of Praise. When we find joy in anything, we want to praise it. But when we also love that which gives us joy, our desire—our *need*—to praise is magnified by the depth of our love. So, when the psalmist says, "I will praise you, LORD, with all my heart" (Psalm 138:1), he's proclaiming the fullness of his love for God, a love that he simply must express in praise to God. The Psalms of Praise thus becomes the psalmists' love poems to God—ones that we can borrow to say, *"I love you, God!"*

In my family we often send greeting cards to our loved ones on birthdays, anniversaries, and holidays, or to celebrate special accomplishments, such as graduations, a new job, or a personal achievement. Whenever I'm in a store looking for a card to send to someone for one of those occasions, I carefully read numerous cards, looking for just the right one. I'll add my own words later, of course, but, still, I'm also relying on the card's words to express my thoughts to the person who will receive it.

The Psalms of Praise work in a similar way to those Hallmark cards—but without the schmaltzy sentiments that characterize too many store-bought cards. They provide me with the words to express my wonder, my gratitude, and my love to God. I may add my own words of praise to God (and I should), but the Psalms of Praise provide a starting place for me.

Since you've made it this far in this book, you know that the psalms are not just religious poems or spiritual pick-me-ups or inspirational sayings. Rather, God intends for the psalms to change us. As we offer the psalms to God as our prayers, our heart slowly changes. Thomas Merton explains the process this way, "As we recite the Psalms, His mysteries are actualized by grace in our own hearts."⁵ As we speak the words of the psalms to God, God graciously speaks those very words into our heart and binds our heart to God's heart a little more tightly.

The Psalms of Praise are especially important in this. As Augustine points out, "God has taught us to praise Him, in the Psalms, not in order that He may get something out of the praise, but in order *that we may be made better by it*."⁶ Through the Praise Psalms we express the wonder, gratitude, and love for God that's already in our heart. But as we pray the praises in the psalms, they gradually become the praises of our own heart—and in the process our heart is transformed. We come to understand more of God's true nature and character, and we grow in our relationship with God. As we learn to praise God, we get to know God better and our joy in God multiplies, which motivates us to praise him even more. Thus the act of praising God creates an ever-expanding cycle of growth and joy and praise.

But praising God is not just for the "here and now" in our life with God. It's also for the "ever and ever" of life with God. To that we must now turn.

Praising God for Ever and Ever

When Emma and I set out on one of our walks, I usually have a destination in mind. Sometimes, it's the park a few blocks down the street. Quite often, it's the meadow in the nature preserve near our home. Occasionally, it's the university where my wife works. While the routes vary from day to day, most of our walks do have a destination; we're not just wandering aimlessly.

That's true for the book of Psalms as well. It, too, has a destination.

Through the different types of psalms, God takes different routes to shape our heart, just as Emma and I take different routes on our walks. So, for instance, God uses the Psalms of Trust to build our faith and confidence in him as we make our way through life. Wisdom Psalms direct us toward wise and faithful living in obedience to God and God's Word. Sacred Story Psalms enable us to find our place in the great Story that God is writing as he creates a people for himself. Psalms of Lament enable us to walk with God as we work through life's disappointments, hurts, and struggles. And Praise Psalms provide us with a means of expressing our wonder, gratitude,

---

5. Merton, *Praying the Psalms*, 18.
6. Merton, *Praying the Psalms*, 12 (emphasis his).

and love to God. As we pray these different types of psalms, God subtly shapes our heart in a multitude of ways.

But, although God's shaping work follows many different routes, God always has a grand, overarching purpose, or destination, in mind. The Apostle Paul reminds us that "it is God who works in you to will and to act in order to fulfill his good purpose" (Phil. 2:13). God has a purpose for each of us. Just as I have a destination in mind when Emma and I set off on one of our holy walks, so God has a destination in mind for each of his people. God is taking us someplace as we journey with him.

The *Westminster Shorter Catechism*[7] refers to that purpose—or destination—in its opening question, "What is the chief concern of human persons?" The Catechism then gives the answer, "The chief human concern is to glorify God and enjoy God forever." That's a wonderfully profound statement about our purpose as human beings. It says that we exist not for ourselves but for God and that our lives should bring honor to the One who created us. But the Catechism also says that, as we live for God and bring honor to God, we experience incredible joy. In other words, life with God is not to be filled with guilt or duty but with boundless love for God and overflowing joy in God. While we only get a taste of that love and joy in our earthly life, it will be full and pure when we're with God for all of eternity.

Psalm 84 helps us imagine that joy of living in God's presence. In this psalm the psalmist envies the swallows and sparrows that have made their nests in the eaves of the temple. He's jealous of them, because they're always in God's presence. Reflecting on those birds, he realizes what a blessing it is to be in God's house, to be in God's presence. But it's a blessing that leads naturally and inevitably to praising God: "Blessed are those who dwell in your house; they are ever praising you" (v. 4). Dwelling in God's presence. Praising God. When we enjoy the blessing of the first, we lovingly engage in the second.

We get a glimpse of what that will be like in the heavenly vision that was given to the Apostle John: "Then I heard every creature in heaven and on earth and under the earth and on the sea, and all that is in them, saying: 'To him who sits on the throne and to the Lamb be praise and honor and glory and power, for ever and ever!'" (Rev. 5:13). That's God's ultimate

---

7. A catechism is a document used for teaching the Christian faith, especially to new converts, and the *Westminster Shorter Catechism* is widely considered to be one of the best summaries of the central teachings of Christianity. It was written in 1646–47 by English and Scottish theologians and laypersons with the purpose of creating a greater theological conformity between the Church of England and the Church of Scotland.

destination for each one of us: that we might join the great chorus of all God's creatures in praising God forever and ever. That's the destination our life journey is preparing us for: to live in God's presence and lovingly and joyfully praise him for ever and ever.

To prepare us for that day, the Psalms—and especially the Psalms of Praise—shape our hearts to know and express our love and joy for God. In this life we get occasional glimpses of God's presence, and we respond with our praises: *Wow, God! Thank You, God! I love you, God!* But so much of the time we aren't conscious of God's presence. Our everyday lives now are filled with challenges and struggles, and many of the psalms help us deal with those, especially the Psalms of Trust and the Psalms of Lament. Those psalms help us live faithfully with God through all the ups and downs of human living. But living with God for all of eternity requires that we learn the language of praise. As we learn to praise God, we become more aware of God's presence, and we become more and more equipped for life in God's presence.

Right now, we're in the first-grade level (or maybe the kindergarten level) of the School of Praise. But one day we'll graduate, and then praising God—expressing our wonder, gratitude, and love to God—will be as natural to us as breathing is for us now. And that's what God's Prayer Book is teaching us to do. The entire book of Psalms is ultimately leading us toward a life of praising God.

We get a hint of this, first of all, in the very title for the book. Although the English title, *The Psalms*, conveys the idea that the psalms are "hymns to be sung to musical accompaniment,"[8] we should recall that the Hebrew title for the book, *Tehillim*, means "Praises." Although the musical dimension is important in the Psalms (and overlooked way too much by this writer), we mustn't lose sight of the emphasis in the original title that the Psalms are, first of all, a collection of "Praises."

The book of Psalms leads us toward praise in a more subtle way as well. Although on first reading the psalms appear to lack any real order, the distribution of the two most-common types of psalms—Laments and Praise Psalms—doesn't seem to be quite so random. In the first three books (Psalms 1–89), Psalms of Lament outnumber Psalms of Praise by more than four to one. However, in the last two books (Psalms 90–150), the Praise Psalms outnumber the Laments by more than two to one.[9] Like

---

8. Harrison, *Old Testament*, 977.

9. Pemberton, *Hurting with God*, 241–6. He categorizes forty-one psalms as Psalms

a teeter totter, the balance between Laments and Praises tilts sharply as we move through the book of Psalms. Increasingly, God's Prayer Book leads us into more and more praise.

This shift towards praise culminates with the final six psalms all being Psalms of Praise. I've already discussed Psalm 145 as being the last psalm attributed to David and his masterpiece of praise to God. But take a moment and skim through Psalms 146–150. As always, I'll still be here when you're done. . . .

Extra Steps:

These five Psalms of Praise (146–150) are quite different from one another. What are some of the differences you observe?

As you skim through these five psalms, try to notice which items of praise make a special impression on you. Then take a moment to reflect on those praises and offer them to God as your own prayers of praise.

As you skimmed through these concluding five psalms, did you notice that each of them begins and ends with "Praise the LORD"? This phrase translates the Hebrew phrase *hallelû-yah* (from which you'll recognize the more familiar form, "Hallelujah"), and for that reason, these last five psalms are often called the "Hallelujah Psalms." However, the word "Hallelujah" isn't just found in these few psalms. In fact, it occurs some twenty-nine times in Psalms 104–150, and various forms of it occur in other places in the Bible as well. For instance, the Greek form of the word occurs four times in Revelation 19, the passage that Handel used as the basis for his *"Hallelujah Chorus."*

Some people are confused by the similarity of "Hallelujah" and "Alleluia." "Hallelujah" is simply a transliteration of the Hebrew into English, but when the Hebrew expression was translated into the Greek Septuagint long ago, the initial "h" sound was dropped. Thus, the Greek form of the word eventually came into English as "Alleluia." So whether we say "Hallelujah" or "Alleluia," we're saying exactly the same thing. The two words are equivalent, and both mean "Praise the Lord!"

---

of Praise and sixty as Psalms of Lament. Only ten (one-fourth) of those Praise Psalms are in Books I–III, compared with forty-seven Psalms of Lament. In Books IV–V, there are thirty-one Praise Psalms and only thirteen Laments.

The Hebrew expression *Hallelû-yah* actually has two parts. *"Hallel"* is a verb that means "praise," and *"Yah"* is a shortened form of God's personal name, Yahweh. Donald Griggs points out that this is a serious word and "should never be uttered lightly. It should be an expression of deep spiritual experience. After all, one is addressing Almighty God, and that is a most serious matter."[10] In this form, *Hallelû-yah* is an imperative, or a command. So when someone says, "Hallelujah!" they're exhorting both themselves and their hearers to engage in the act of praising God.

That's what these final Hallelujah Psalms are doing. In various ways, each of them summons us to offer our praises to God. Together, they create a tremendous crescendo of praise for God as God's Prayer Book draws to a close. As Eugene Peterson observes, "The five hallelujah psalms with Psalm 145 as a foundation are a cathedral built entirely of praise."[11]

Psalm 150, the fifth of these Hallelujah Psalms and the very last psalm in the book of Psalms, is especially significant in that respect. In fact, it might be considered the epitome of Praise Psalms, since *every line* begins with the word "praise." In six short verses, this psalm tells us *where* we should praise God (in his sanctuary and in his mighty heavens), *what* we should praise God for (his acts of power and his surpassing greatness), and *how* we should praise God (exuberantly, with dancing, and with all kinds of musical instruments). The final verse gathers up all this praise for God and says, "Let everything that has breath praise the Lord. Hallelujah!" Thus the very last words in the book of Psalms are a call for everyone and everything to praise God.

So that's the destination the Psalms are leading us towards. We may begin our prayers by hoping God will give us the good things we desire. Or that God will fix whatever bad situation we're in. Or we may be venting our complaints to God, like in the Laments. We have all kinds of motivations for praying. Our prayers *begin* in all kinds of places. But as we learn to pray, as we learn God's language of prayer, this is the place we're ultimately led. We're led into the praise of God. We may not begin with praising God, but that's where we end up. In the final analysis, God's Prayer Book teaches us to praise God and "to enjoy God forever."

As I recounted in chapter 1, my journey in God's Prayer Book began when I became convicted that my prayer life was long on asking God for stuff and short on praising God for who God is and what God's done. I was treating God like a cosmic Amazon.com: I just typed in my request, hit the

---

10. Griggs, *Psalms – Resource Book*, 80.
11. Peterson, *Answering God*, 127.

order button, and my prayer was on its way to God. Then I'd wait to receive my answer back from God, preferably via overnight shipping. I knew that wasn't the way prayer should be, but that's what I had slipped into.

Then my devotional reading led me to Psalm 145, and to verse 2 in particular, which says: "Every day I will praise you and extol your name for ever and ever." As I reflected on that verse, I was struck by the combination of "every day" and "for ever and ever" in David's commitment to praising God. For David, praising God was both a daily discipline and a lifelong (and eternal) practice.

I immediately realized that this was what had been missing in my prayer life. While I pray in some way every day, I knew that most of my prayers focused on my needs or the needs of others. I didn't often take the time to stop and reflect on God's name and God's character and all that God's done for me and for the world.

Recognizing that shortcoming in my prayer life was one of the reasons I decided to memorize Psalm 145 and make it one of my regular prayers. For a long time I prayed it every day. Now that I've learned many other psalms, I pray it less often, but it's still among my favorites and a wonderful way for me to express my joy to God. As I pray it, I also find my joy and my love for God increase as well. No matter what frustrations I'm feeling or struggles I'm wrestling with, whenever I pray this psalm, my attitude shifts a little. I smile—at least for a moment. I experience a bit of God's love and joy. And my heart moves a little closer to that day when I'll know the joy of praising God "for ever and ever."

That was the start of my journey into the Psalms, but, as we've seen, in many ways that's also the destination for my journey—for *our* journeys: learning to praise God "every day for ever and ever." I'm certainly not there yet, but as I've learned to include more praise in my prayer life, I've found that prayer has taken on a different feel for me. Now I sense that I'm truly praying to my heavenly Father, not just sending requests off to some celestial clearinghouse. Here's the prayer I wrote in my journal after reflecting on that verse. May this be your prayer as well:

> *Gracious God, you are indeed worthy of my praise, not just on occasion, but all the time, every day. I would like to make it a habit to praise you for something every day. So teach me to do that. May your Spirit fill my mind with thoughts of you, and may my mouth speak forth your praises when I'm by myself and when I'm with others. May you take great delight and be honored by my praise. For I pray this in Jesus' name, Amen.*

Extra Steps:

What do you think it means to praise God?

How would you explain to a child or to a non-believer what praising God is all about?

As you reflect on the Psalms of Praise, what have you learned that will help you in praising God?

Chapter 9

A Panoramic View

*"I lift up my eyes to the mountains—
where does my help come from?
My help comes from the L*ORD*,
the Maker of heaven and earth."*

—PSALM 121:1-2

WHEN EMMA AND I go for one of our holy walks in the nature preserve near our home, we usually follow paths through the lower meadow. We meander along, observing (or in Emma's case, sniffing) the wildflowers, the grasses, the trees, and the occasional critter. Once in a while, however, we take a trail that climbs up the side of the bluff and overlooks the meadow.

As we walk along that upper trail, I can see the spider web of paths that crisscross the meadow down below us. Off in the distance, several high-rise buildings remind me that I'm actually not all that far from civilization, even though it can feel that way here in the nature preserve. Farther away still, the horizon is outlined by numerous mountains, including Mt. Spokane, which is the highest peak around here.

I really enjoy the different perspective of that panoramic view. On most of our walks, I observe things up close. But once in a while it's good to draw back and see the big picture. That's what I aim to do in this chapter. So far in this journey through the Psalms, I've looked "up close" at topics such as prayer-walking, heart-learning, conversing with God, Hebrew poetry, and five key types of psalms. But now I want to wrestle with a "big picture" question: *As we learn and pray the Psalms, is there a panoramic, or overarching, theme in what God's Prayer Book teaches us? And, if so, what is it?*

A short answer to that question is that the Psalms teach us about God. Of course, they don't give us a comprehensive theology lesson like we might receive in a systematic theology course. Nor do they employ the formal language so often used to describe the attributes of God: omniscient, omnipresent, and so forth. No, what we learn about God in the Psalms is enormously personal and relational. As we pray them, we discover that the Psalms are not teaching us *about* God so much as they're teaching us to *know* God, they're drawing us into a deeper and more vibrant relationship with God.

We can describe that relationship in many ways, of course, just as we can our other relationships. For instance, as Carol's husband, I could be described as her lover, as her best friend, and as her life partner. Each of those descriptions/titles adds something important to your understanding of my relationship with Carol. Together, they provide a deeper insight into what being her husband is all about. They enrich the meaning of my relationship with Carol in a way that "husband" by itself cannot.

Similarly, just referring to God as "God" tells us very little about the relationship we have (or don't have) with him. After all, people have all kinds of conceptions about what "God" means. However, we can illuminate God's relationship with us by using three titles for God: *Creator*, *Leader*, and *Rescuer*. Seeing God as our Creator, our Leader, and our Rescuer leads us into a richer understanding of the nature of God's relationship with us, and those three dimensions of God's relationship with his people are knit into the very fabric of the Psalms. Indeed, it's impossible to understand the Psalms without seeing God in these three ways. For that reason, in this chapter, I'll unpack what the Psalms teach us about each of these titles, and I'll help us consider some implications they have for our lives. So, let's jump into this panoramic view of the Psalms and explore these dimensions of God's relationship with us.

Extra Steps:

Before you read my thoughts on what the Psalms teach us, take a few moments and reflect on what you've been learning about God in your own study of the Psalms. In what ways have the Psalms enlarged or changed your understanding of God?

What aspects of God's relationship with you are especially meaningful at this time in your life?

God as Our Creator

Numerous psalms make reference in various ways to God as the Creator. For example, Psalm 102:25 describes God's work in creating the earth and the heavens; Psalm 74:16–17 refers to God creating the seasons; and Psalm 24:1–2 affirms that, since God created everything, it all belongs to God: "The earth is the LORD's, and everything in it, the world and all who live in it; for he founded it on the seas and established it on the waters." In addition, Psalm 95:6 refers to God as "our Maker," and Psalm 149:2 says Israel should "rejoice in their Maker."

On several occasions, God is referred to as "the Maker of heaven and earth" (see Psalms 115:15, 121:2, 124:8, 134:3, and 146:6). The phrase "heaven and earth" is an example of a *merism*: a figure of speech in which a pair of contrasting words are used to represent a totality. So, as a merism, the expression "heaven and earth" is not referring to two locations but rather to *all* that exists. Saying that God is the Maker of heaven and earth is simply a poetic way of acknowledging God as the Creator of everything that exists—seen and unseen, physical and spiritual.

Another example of a merism is in Psalm 139:2 ("You know when I sit and when I rise"), where the two actions of sitting and rising are used to indicate that God knows *everything* the psalmist does. The merism, "alpha and omega" (the first and last letters of the Greek alphabet), refers to the beginning and the ending—as well as everything in between (see Rev. 22:13). A common merism is when we say that something is covered "from A to Z." That's a way of saying it's completely and totally covered.

The theme of God as Creator, as the Maker of heaven and earth, is woven throughout God's Prayer Book. However, five psalms go beyond simply referring to God's role as the Creator and actually center in on this dimension of God's relationship to the world and to us. These five *Creation Psalms* are Psalms 8, 19, 104, 139, and 148. These psalms all focus on God's role as the Creator of all that exists, although each provides a slightly different emphasis.

Of these five Creation Psalms, my favorite is Psalm 104. I first got acquainted with this psalm while attending a retreat led by the Old Testament scholar Walter Brueggemann. During the retreat, Dr. Brueggemann led us in several hours of discussion on this psalm, and I came to appreciate it so much. (Dr. Brueggemann also made numerous other Old Testament passages come alive with his insights. It should come as no surprise that several of his books are listed in the bibliography at the end of this book.)

Before I discuss what Psalm 104 says about God as our Creator, why don't you take a few minutes and read through it yourself? As you read, notice the words or phrases that jump out to you, as well as the thoughts that the psalm sparks in your mind. Go ahead, I'll wait here for you.

* * *

What were your impressions of this psalm? What did you notice about it?

One of the first things I noticed is the wide variety of animals that are mentioned: wild donkeys, birds, storks, goats, hyrax (a small, weasel-like mammal), lions, and sea creatures. For that reason I often think of this as "the zoo psalm." Continuing in that vein, we're told that God created springs, trees, and mountains as habitats for these creatures, and that God provides for them much as a zookeeper provides for his or her menagerie. As an unapologetic animal lover, I greatly appreciate this aspect of Psalm 104. God the Zookeeper!

Of course, Psalm 104 teaches us much more about God's work as Creator than just his love for animals. In poetic language the psalm also describes God's original work in creating the world and all that exists. So, God "stretches out the heavens like a tent" (v. 2), "sets the earth on its foundations" (v. 5), "makes springs pour water into the ravines" (v. 10), and makes the moon and the sun (v. 19). God is also seen as imposing order on the created world by establishing the seasons, as well as night and day (vv. 19–23). Although the psalm lacks the ordered structure of the creation account in Genesis 1, the purpose is much the same: to affirm that everything that exists comes from the powerful hands of God himself. This lengthy psalm celebrates the way all of creation—animals, humans, weather, and seasons—owes its existence to God and takes its direction from God.

Of course, like with Genesis 1, we should not read these descriptions through the eyes of modern science. Neither the psalmist nor the writer of Genesis is attempting to explain the "how" of creation (certainly not in a way that would satisfy our scientific minds). Rather, by using an image like putting on a garment (v. 6), the psalmist is indicating how *easily* God created all that exists. God expended no more effort in covering the world with water (oceans, seas, lakes, etc.) than you or I would in putting on a sweater. Through images like this the psalmist focuses our attention on God's power and sovereignty over all of creation.

This is probably the purpose behind the reference to "Leviathan" in verse 26. Elsewhere in the Bible, as well as in ancient mythologies, Leviathan is viewed as a fearsome sea monster (see Job 41 and Isa. 27:1). This was one of the reasons why the sea itself was viewed as such a threat by the ancient peoples. Leviathan represented chaos and disorder similar to that described in Genesis 1:2. In ancient creation myths, the gods Marduk (Babylonian) and Baal (Canaanite) had to wrestle and defeat Leviathan in order to create the world, their victories being symbolic of overcoming chaos. In stark contrast, however, Psalm 104 shows Leviathan as having been created by God and completely under God's control. The *NIV* translation says God formed Leviathan "to frolic" in the sea. Brueggemann expands on that image, saying that Leviathan is pictured here as having been created by God "for sport" and as causing God to "laugh in delight."[1] The great fearsome monster is simply a household pet for the God who created the universe.

In addition to God's work of creating all that exists, the psalm also affirms God's role in maintaining and providing for his creation, a kind of ongoing creative work. We see this, for example, in the way God causes springs to bring water to the animals, provides grass for the cattle and food for people (v. 14), and gives food to all the creatures (the lions, specifically, in v. 21 but all creatures in v. 27). It's important to notice, however, that God goes beyond just meeting the basic needs of his creatures. God also gives them an abundant and joyful life through such means as providing "wine that gladdens human hearts" (v. 15) and satisfying his creatures with "good things" (v. 28). The Creator is a *good* Creator who truly cares for his creatures and his creation.

Psalm 139, another Creation Psalm, personalizes this theme of God as Creator. In this psalm God is not primarily viewed as the Creator of all that exists—although that's assumed, since there's no place in all of creation to which the psalmist could ever flee from God's presence (vv. 7–12). Instead, God is seen as having personally created the psalmist. "You knit me together in my mother's womb," the psalmist declares (v. 13).

This personalizing of creation in Psalm 139 is similar to the second creation account in Genesis 2, in which God is said to have formed the man out of the dust of the ground (Gen. 2:7). Instead of simply speaking human beings into existence like God did in the first creation account (Gen. 1:27), God creates the man like a potter might create something out of clay. Then, using a divine form of CPR, God breathes life into the man. Shortly after that, God becomes an anesthesiologist/surgeon and fashions the first woman from one of the man's ribs (vv. 21–22). Through such images, Genesis 2

---

1. Brueggemann, *No Secrets*, 61.

reveals the personal and intimate side of God as Creator in much the same way that Psalm 139 does.

In Psalm 139 the psalmist realizes that God's intimate knowledge of the psalmist goes well beyond the acts of knitting him together in his mother's womb or seeing his unformed body (vv. 13–16). Indeed, the psalmist notes that God's knowledge of the psalmist also extends to all of his thoughts, words, and actions (vv. 1–4). Even more, God has planned out all the days of the psalmist's life (v. 16). Truly, God knows the psalmist inside and out.

From the perspective of Psalm 139, then, everything about us has been lovingly and personally formed by our Creator. Yes, the psalmist affirms that God is the Creator of all that exists, but, more significantly, he celebrates God as *his own personal Creator*. In other words, God didn't just create *people*. God created *me*. And *you*. And *each* person. Individually. With love. And with full knowledge of precisely what he was doing. Wow, God! Praise be to you!

Extra Steps:

Examine the other three Creation Psalms (8, 19, and 148) for yourself, looking for what they add to your understanding of God as Creator:

Compare Psalms 8 and 19. Both say that creation reveals the Creator in various ways. How is that revelation similar in each psalm, and how is it different? In what ways have you personally learned about God from the world around you?

What does Psalm 148 emphasize in its description of God as Creator? What response does this psalm call for?

When we talk about God as Creator, we sometimes get caught up in issues such as creation-versus-evolution, the age of the universe, or where dinosaurs fit into the creation narrative. But the psalmists were never especially interested in *how* God created everything. Nor did they know anything about dinosaurs or modern astrophysics. Rather, their descriptions of God's creative activities are clearly poetical: "he stretches out the heavens like a tent" (Psalm 104:2), and personal: "let us kneel before the Lord our Maker" (Psalm 95:6). For them, the important thing is that God *is* our Creator.

As you reflect on that last statement, allow me to suggest several implications this might have for our lives. What does it mean for us that God is the One who created us (as well as everything else around us)?

First of all, acknowledging God as the Creator of all that exists reminds us of our proper place in the universe. We are the creatures, not the Creator—contrary to what we often like to imagine. Each of us is utterly dependent upon God for our very life: for every breath we take, every thought we have, every word we speak, and every action we take. None of that would be possible if it weren't for the gracious and loving power of our Creator. Sin arises whenever we forget this basic truth, so praying the Creation Psalms is a good way to remember that God is God and we are not.

But knowing our proper place also means knowing we're loved by our Creator. We were created to be in a personal and intimate relationship with the One who made us. That's the clear teaching of Psalm 139, as we noted above, but it echoes throughout the Psalms. God is a covenant-making God who desires to be in a relationship with us. And so, as our Creator, God fashioned each of us personally and individually—which means that nothing about us is hidden from him. God knows all about us, yet he continues to love us, provide for us, and rescue us. What an amazing Creator!

Second, since God created everything, God owns it all, as Psalm 24:1 reminds us. This means we're in the world as guests and caretakers, not as owners or masters. Thus, we have a responsibility to be good caretakers of the physical environment around us. Psalm 65 (the "eco-psalm," as I think of it) celebrates the way God takes care of his creation: "You care for the land and water it; you enrich it abundantly" (v. 9). Then the last several verses recount some of the ways God has enriched the world around us. The point seems obvious. If God is so concerned about his creation, shouldn't we be also?

In addition to our responsibility to care for the physical world, we also need to care for every person, since each of them also belongs to the Creator. We need to look out for others and interact with them like the Creator does: with generosity, love, mercy, and justice. Psalm 15 asks the question, "LORD, who may dwell in your sacred tent? Who may live on your holy mountain?" The answer is given in a litany of actions and attitudes, most of which focus on how we treat others. Acknowledging our Creator ought to shape the way we treat the people God has created.

Third, creation teaches us about the Creator. As Psalms 8 and 19 tell us, we can learn much about God simply by observing his creation. The

Apostle Paul makes this same point in Romans 1:20, "For since the creation of the world God's invisible qualities—his eternal power and divine nature—have been clearly seen, being understood from what has been made." Creation certainly doesn't teach us everything we need to know about God, but perhaps some things can only be learned (or be *best* learned) from the created world. For example, who can doubt the Creator's power when they're watching the waters thunder over Niagara Falls? Who won't appreciate God's care for the tiniest things when they observe a beautiful butterfly up close? And who hasn't been overwhelmed by the Creator's glory made manifest in a stunning sunset? The artwork reveals the Artist, and the created world is God's canvas.

Unfortunately, as Calvin Miller observes, many of us have made God into an "inside God." We only think about God when we're in a church sanctuary or a private study. The effect of this is that our God shrinks. However, the outdoors world provides a correction to this, as Miller explains:

> Our inside God is too small. We need to view him through the universe he created. Then he will be elevated to his exalted place. . . . A supersized God makes us aware of our smallness and our humble place in the universe. . . . Once we have seen the God of Yosemite and the Everglades, we will be better able to celebrate his awesome reality and our hearts will overflow with praise.[2]

In other words, creation points us to the Creator, to a *big* Creator! And that leads us into praise and worship of the Creator, which is the final implication flowing from God being our Creator. When we consider the kind of Creator our God is, and when we behold the wonder and magnificence of God's creation, how can we not be drawn into greater praise and worship? Creation reveals a Creator who is powerful, artistic, awesome, beautiful, and purposeful. A Creator who loves and cares for his creation and for the people he created. No wonder the book of Psalms ends with the exhortation, "Let everything that has breath praise the Lord. Praise the Lord!" (150:6). *Wholehearted worship* is the proper response to our loving and all-powerful Creator. How could we respond with anything less?

Extra Steps:

Take a walk outside and try to see some things you've never noticed before. What do those observations reveal to you about your

2. Miller, *Celtic Prayer*, 104–5.

> *Creator? As you walk, allow the outdoors to be your sanctuary and imagine God's presence all around you. Tell God what his being your Creator means to you.*

God as Our Leader

As we continue with our panoramic overview of the Psalms, we notice that God the Creator didn't finish creating the universe and then run off to get started on some other divine project. Rather, the Creator remained personally involved with his creation and with the people he created. Indeed, God created us for that very reason: so that we could be in a *relationship* with him.

That relationship is never one of equals, of course, since the creature can never be equal to the Creator (as we noted above). Instead, the Psalms show God relating to his people in numerous ways that leave no doubt about who's in charge. Some of those ways include God ruling over, commanding, teaching, directing, guiding, and judging his people. In all of those ways (and others), God is the one who is leading, and the people are obeying, responding, and following. "Leader" is a title that incorporates all of those actions and describes God's *ongoing* relationship with us. In other words, God is both our Creator and our Leader.

As far as I can find, God is specifically called our Leader just once in the entire Bible. That's in 2 Chronicles 13:12, where Abijah, the king of Judah, tells the rebellious king, Jeroboam, "God is with us; he is our leader." However, there are many verses in the Psalms where God is asked to lead us. Consider these examples:

- "*Lead* me, Lord, in your righteousness because of my enemies—make your way straight before me" (Psalm 5:8).
- "Teach me your way, Lord; *lead* me in a straight path because of my oppressors" (Psalm 27:11).
- "Since you are my rock and my fortress, for the sake of your name *lead* and guide me" (Psalm 31:3).
- "See if there is any offensive way in me, and *lead* me in the way everlasting" (Psalm 139:24).
- "Teach me to do your will, for you are my God; may your good Spirit *lead* me on level ground" (Psalm 143:10).

As we can see even in this small sampling, the psalmists looked to God to lead them in a variety of ways. For instance, in these five verses alone we see God leading the psalmists by teaching, by guiding, and by judging. These verses, and many others, show us that God's ongoing relationship with the people he created is one of divine leadership.

Extra Steps:

Think of several people whom you consider to be (or to have been) great leaders. How did they exercise their leadership? In what ways did their leadership differ from each other?

What thoughts and images come to your mind when you think about God as your Leader? This may be a new concept for you. If so, do you think this is a good title for how God relates to you, and why or why not? Can you come up with another title to describe this leadership dimension of God's relationship with his people?

Although the psalmists don't call God their "Leader," they do make frequent use of two titles, or metaphors, that emphasize God's leadership. These are *King* and *Shepherd*.

God is addressed as "King" more than twenty times in the book of Psalms, and there are additional references to God's royal "throne." Indeed, we might well have entitled this second section "God our King" instead of "God our Leader." However, I didn't do that for three reasons. One is that King is a bit of a foreign term for many of us. Another is that Leader has no gender implied. And the third—and most important—reason is that Leader is a broader title than King and includes some aspects of God's relationship with us that King doesn't. We'll consider some of those other aspects shortly, but first let's explore the nature of God's kingship by examining a couple of short psalms. Take a few moments to read Psalms 47 and 98 and notice especially what each one says about God as our King. As always, I'll wait right here for you. (I haven't gone away yet, have I?)

* * *

What did you notice in Psalm 47? What stands out to me is how this psalm celebrates God as the King over all the nations, not just Israel. The psalm is addressed to "all you nations" (v. 1), claims that God "reigns over the nations" (v. 8), and states that all the kings of the earth belong to God (v. 9). No wonder the psalmist can refer to God as "the great King over all the earth" (vv. 2 and 7). In the eyes of this psalmist, God is truly the King of kings.

These affirmations show us that God's kingship is universal, even though Longman rightly calls this "an act of theological imagination," since none of those other kings would have acknowledged Israel's God as the King over their part of the world.[3] Nevertheless, this psalm asserts that God *is* on his throne, reigning over all the nations, even when people don't realize it (vv. 8–9). In other words, we don't make God our King in the way we might elect someone to be our president. No, God is our King *because God has chosen to be our King*. This is one of the key ways God the Creator has chosen to lead and relate to the people he created.

However, God's kingship is not ceremonial or honorific. The fact that God the King is reigning over all the nations underscores God's supreme authority, and God manifests that regal authority by issuing decrees and edicts for his people to follow. In other words, the King is the Ruler, who leads by giving commands and teaching us his laws. In his capacity as Ruler, God the King makes it clear how he expects us to live, and as the King's subjects, we have the duty to obey all of his laws and edicts.

This responsibility to follow our King's ways is especially emphasized in the Wisdom and Torah Psalms, which I talked about in chapter 6. Through these psalms especially, we're summoned to meditate on God's law (Psalm 1:2), we ask God to teach us his ways (Psalm 119:33), and we recommit ourselves to being God's obedient followers (Psalm 119:34). We can pray like that, because our King's laws are not burdens imposed on us by some sovereign whim. Instead, since our King is also our Creator, he fully knows how we were designed and made. He knows what's best for us, and his laws and commands reflect that. They're the means through which we can know the life our Creator intended for us. When we realize that, we can eagerly join with the psalmist in pleading to our King, "Be gracious to me and teach me your law" (Psalm 119:29). May we always delight in knowing and following the ways of our King.

Like all kings, however, God the King expects his subjects to obey his decrees and to follow his ways. They're not optional. As Psalm 119:4 affirms: "You have laid down precepts that are to be fully obeyed." And when those commands are not obeyed, judgment necessarily follows. The King becomes the Judge. In ancient times, ruling and judging usually were not separated like they are in our day. Instead, kings also acted as judges

---

3. Longman III, *Psalms (TOTC)*, 209.

and were always the final court of appeal—that was just part of their kingly authority. So when the Psalms speak of God as the Judge, they're affirming another aspect of God's authority as the King.

We see this, for example, in Psalm 98. In verse 6 the whole earth is called to "shout for joy before the Lord, the King." Then the entire physical world (the sea, rivers, and mountains) is summoned to sing praises to God. Finally, the psalm ends by stating that this King will come "to judge the earth. He will judge the world in righteousness and the peoples with equity." As the King who also judges, God will summon all people to a divine judgment, one that is based on righteousness and equity, on justice and fairness.

In judging us, God is holding us accountable for our obedience—or lack thereof—to his laws and commands. However, God's intent is not to condemn the disobedient. After all, God's the Creator who made us and who loves every single one of us. God wants the disobedient and the unfaithful to turn back to his ways. Yet, our actions and choices eventually have consequences. To see how seriously the King views ongoing disobedience and unfaithfulness, take a moment and look up these verses: Psalms 34:16; 73:18–19, 27; 95:8–11; and 145:20.

* * *

Knowing that the King is the Judge should prompt us to examine our own faithfulness. A great example of this is the end of Psalm 139 where the psalmist actually invites God to judge him: "Search me, God, and know my heart; test me and know my anxious thoughts. See if there is any offensive way in me, and lead me in the way everlasting" (vv. 23–24). The psalmist desperately wants to walk in God's way, and so he asks God to do a "performance review" on him. He wants God to let him know how he's doing and where he needs to improve or change. This is a wonderfully healthy view of God as our Judge. The King judges us so that we can become more like the people he wants us to be. Therefore, we look to our King to judge us by holding us accountable and revealing those areas where we need to grow or change.

Another way that the King acts as Judge involves defending the powerless and those who are victims of evildoers. In the Psalms, as in the rest of Scripture, God the Judge actively sides with the innocent and the helpless. As Psalm 103:6 puts it, "The Lord works righteousness and justice for all the oppressed." An example of this is in Psalm 10:14–16, where wicked people had been afflicting others, but the psalmist knows that God sees "the trouble of the afflicted" and is "the helper of the fatherless." So he urges God to "call the evildoer to account for his wickedness." In verse 16, he addresses God as "the King for ever and ever." Because the Judge and the King are one and the same, he pleads for the King to step in as the Judge and act on behalf of those victims.

To recap, we've seen that the title, King, says much about how God relates to us. As the King, God rules over all the nations and all people, commands us to obey his laws and walk in his ways, and serves as the Judge to ensure that his ways are followed. Those are all important ways that God leads us as our King.

However, calling God our Leader involves more than just those kingly qualities. To see this, we need to consider another title, or metaphor, that the psalmists use for God: *Shepherd*.

In contrast to the wide-spread use of "King" as a divine title, the psalmists directly call God their "Shepherd" only three times. The best-known instance of this is Psalm 23:1, where David testifies, "The LORD is my Shepherd." In addition, God is addressed as the "Shepherd of Israel" in Psalm 80:1, and Psalm 28:9 ends with a plea for God to "be their shepherd and carry them forever."

Although the *title* "Shepherd" is used sparingly, God's *role* as Shepherd is assumed on a number of other occasions where God's people are referred to as "sheep" or as a "flock" in God's "pasture." For examples of God's assumed role as our Shepherd, see Psalms 37:3, 74:1, 78:52, 79:13, 95:7, and 119:76. An especially good illustration of this is Psalm 100:3: "Know that the LORD is God. It is he who made us, and we are his; we are his people, the sheep of his pasture." Here the psalmist picks up one of our earlier themes: that we belong to God because God created us. Then he expands on that by saying we're not just people who belong to the Creator but sheep in God's pasture. In other words, God our Creator is also God our Shepherd.

Today, if we were to list different kinds of leaders, shepherds probably wouldn't even make the Top 100. In Old Testament times, however, "shepherd" was a common metaphor for the kings of Israel (and for kings in other parts of the Ancient Near East as well). Kings were frequently portrayed as shepherds of God's people, and ruling was akin to shepherding.[4] An example of this—albeit a negative one—is in Ezekiel 34, where God condemned "the shepherds of Israel" (the kings) for their failures

---

4. See Longman III, *Psalms (TOTC)*, 134.

to take care of their "flock" (God's people, the Israelites). After rebuking Israel's negligent shepherds, God then promised what he would do as the Shepherd of his people.

The leadership dimension of God's shepherding is explicitly mentioned in both Psalms 23 and 80, which I referred to above. After affirming God's role as his Shepherd in Psalm 23, David cites several shepherding actions that God does on his behalf, including: "he *leads* me beside quiet waters" (v. 2). In Psalm 80, when the psalmist prays to the Shepherd of Israel, he adds, "you who *lead* Joseph like a flock" (v. 1). In addition, Psalm 78, one of the Sacred Story Psalms, uses the image of a shepherd leading his sheep when it recalls the Exodus and Israel's wilderness wandering: "But he brought his people out like a flock; he *led* them like sheep through the wilderness" (v. 52).

These examples show that calling God our Shepherd affirms God's divine leadership just as much as the title King does. However, God exercises his leadership differently as our Shepherd than he does as our King. To see what the Shepherd's leadership encompasses, let's take a closer look at David's "Shepherd Psalm," Psalm 23. Before we do that, take a moment to read through that psalm, preferably in a translation you don't normally use. Because this psalm is so familiar to many of us, we often gloss over its words and expressions without much thought. Reading it in a different version can yield fresh insights into this old favorite. I personally appreciate the *New Living Translation's* rendition, and you might give that a look. (A helpful resource for this is www.BibleGateway.com.) As you read this psalm, ask yourself what makes it so beloved for so many people. Once again, I'll wait right here for you.

* * *

So why do you think this psalm is so special for so many of us?

I suspect the popularity of Psalm 23 has much to do with the warm intimacy between David and his Shepherd. David begins this Psalm of Trust (see chapter 6) by declaring, "The LORD is *my* shepherd" (italics added). There's something deeply personal in that affirmation. David continues to display that sense of intimacy as he describes all that his Shepherd does for him: leading him to green pastures where he can graze and eat his fill and to peaceful streams where he'll have all the water he needs, refreshing his soul (the *New Living Translation* says, "he renews my strength"), and guiding him along the right paths in life. No wonder David can say in verse 1, "I lack nothing" (*NLT*: "I have everything I need"). The picture David lays out is one of his Shepherd personally ensuring that he has everything he needs in life.

In verse 5 David views his Shepherd as a table host. A good host prepares the feast, anoints his guest with the traditional oils, and makes sure the guest's cup is always full and overflowing—and that's what the Shepherd does for David. Such a feast is a picture of close intimacy, as eating together generally is. It's also a picture of abundance and blessing. The Shepherd/Host goes well beyond just meeting the essential needs referred to in verse 1.

In the final verse David affirms his confidence that God's "goodness and unfailing love will pursue me all the days of my life." Thinking of the shepherd imagery once again, Longman suggests that "goodness and love act like the shepherd's sheepdogs, helping the shepherd to keep the sheep going in the right direction."[5] David sees his Shepherd leading him and guiding him even to the very end of his life.

So the intimacy of David's relationship with God is one reason this psalm is so beloved. Perhaps another is that David doesn't sugarcoat life's difficult times but, rather, affirms God's gracious presence even in the midst of those hard times. He says he can courageously face even the darkest valleys in life, because he knows his Shepherd will be there with him (v. 4). And even when he's surrounded by enemies, God will still provide abundantly for him (v. 5).

As we reflect on David's portrait of his Shepherd, we begin to see other aspects of God's leadership, in addition to the ways God leads us as our King.

The first is that, as our Shepherd, God's leadership is deeply personal. While one might affirm God as "*my* King," that's more a statement of loyalty than of intimacy. Kings lead from their thrones. They issue their decrees, and they pass their judgments. A shepherd, however, is out in the field with his sheep. He walks alongside them, personally guiding them to the right places. He uses his staff to gently direct them and his club to beat off predators. He binds up any wounds the sheep may suffer and willingly gets their dirt and blood on himself. Throughout it all, he's intimately involved with his sheep in a way that a king most likely is not with his subjects. So, when David says, "The LORD is my Shepherd," he's describing a close and personal relationship.

---

5. Longman III, *Psalms (TOTC)*, 137.

While a king leads by issuing commands, God leads us as our Shepherd by carefully guiding us along our life's journey. The Shepherd grants us great freedom to roam and wander, but his staff always pulls us back from danger and makes sure we're going in the right direction. As our Shepherd God knows what we need, and so he leads us to those green pastures and peaceful streams. God gently guides us to places that'll satisfy us and meet our needs.

As he leads us through life, God also watches over us as a shepherd watches over his flock, protecting us and caring for us. As David reminds us, no valley is too dark for our Shepherd and no enemy is too overwhelming. Therefore, like David, we can walk in secure confidence, knowing that the Shepherd's watchful eyes are always looking out for us.

When we call God our Leader, we need to remember these leadership qualities of a shepherd as well. As our Shepherd, God leads us by being personally and intimately involved in our lives, by guiding us through life, and by providing for us and protecting us. This isn't leadership from on high; it's leadership in the trenches, in the meadows and the valleys and the hillsides. It's the loving presence and leadership of God our Shepherd, who is always walking with us.

Extra Steps:

In John 10:1–18 Jesus refers to himself as the Good Shepherd and his followers as his sheep. Read through that passage and note the qualities that make for a good shepherd, according to Jesus. How does Jesus' understanding of his shepherd role compare with what David affirms about God as his (and our) Shepherd in Psalm 23?

So that's the second way the Psalms show God relating to us: as our Leader. God leads us like a king (by issuing commands and decrees, teaching us his ways, and holding us accountable to obey those royal edicts and laws), and God also leads us like a shepherd (by maintaining a personal relationship with each of us and by guiding us, providing for us, and protecting us).

Earlier, we said that *wholehearted worship* is our proper response to God as our Creator: we should give ourselves in wonder and praise to the One who created us. The way we should respond to God as our Leader is with *faithful obedience*. God expects nothing less than total obedience from us. All the time. In every situation. That's how we follow our Leader: by constantly striving to live in faithful obedience.

Of course, we don't do that perfectly. Sheep sometimes (often?) go astray and wander off, or they get attacked by wild animals, or thieves try to steal them. But when that happens, the shepherd assumes another role: rescuer. The shepherd does whatever's necessary to rescue his sheep. And this brings us to the third way the Psalms show God relating to us and being active in our lives. God's our Creator. God's our Leader. But God's also our Rescuer, the one who helps us and saves us in so many situations.

God as Our Rescuer

Last year I picked up a second walking companion. Her name is Bella, and, like Emma, she's a beautiful, orange-and-white Brittany Spaniel. She's also full of puppy energy and still needs to learn how to walk nicely. For that reason, prayer walks with Bella are still somewhat of a challenge. However, one recent walk turned into an adventure for a different reason.

Walking along, Bella and I passed by a home with a fenced front yard and a sign that read, "Beware of Dog." Inside the yard, a large, gray-brown Weimaraner watched us carefully. Obviously, that was the dog referred to in the warning. He didn't look especially scary however. He didn't growl or seem at all nervous about our presence. So I didn't give him a second thought, and we continued on our way.

A while later, our return route took us back by that same house. This time, however, the Weimaraner was sitting *outside* the fence. I have no idea how he got out, but there he was, sitting calmly, once again eying us as we walked by—but now without any barrier separating him from us. Suddenly, like a sprinter breaking out of his starting blocks, the dog raced the short distance towards us. Before I could react, he jumped on Bella, knocking her down. His jaws opened wide on the back of her neck. . . .

Dogs often say hi to Emma and Bella when we're on our walks. Sometimes they'll bark at us, and I imagine them pleading, "Can I come with you? Can I? Can I?" If they get the opportunity, the dogs will sniff each other—usually with tails going full-speed and a body language that says, "Oh, goody! A new friend!"

But this Weimaraner showed no sign of friendliness as he pounced on Bella.

As soon as I grasped what was happening, I kicked the attacking dog in the side—*hard!*—and prepared to do it again. But that one kick was enough. The dog backed off and slunk over by the fence. Fortunately, Bella wasn't hurt, and we quickly resumed our walk—although I kept looking over my shoulder for quite some time.

In all the dog-walking I've done, that's the only close encounter I've ever had with a vicious dog. However, that one encounter likely would have ended very badly if I hadn't come to Bella's rescue. I haven't had to be a rescuer very often during my 60-plus years of life, but I'm very thankful I was able to do that when it was necessary.

Rescuing Bella from that Weimaraner makes me think about all the times God has rescued *me*. God's never had to rescue me from an aggressive dog, but, occasionally, God's saved me from the attacks of enemies or the evil one. Often, God's delivered me from myself: from dumb things I've done or from my own willful disobedience. I suspect God's also protected me from all kinds of troubles that I'm not even aware of. That's just what God does. In fact, we might even say that God is in the "rescue business."

From beginning to end, the book of Psalms proclaims this theme of God rescuing his people. Psalm 1 notes that "the LORD watches over the way of the righteous" (v. 6). Here, I picture God as a loving parent, keeping a watchful eye on his or her children, making sure they're safe and protected. At the very end of the Psalter, Psalm 150 praises God for "his acts of power" (v. 2), which surely includes all of those rescues and acts of deliverance along life's journey. In between those two psalms, many, many others refer to God rescuing, saving, delivering, guarding, protecting, or redeeming people. We don't have to search very hard to see God relating to his people as their Rescuer.

To help you appreciate just how prevalent this theme is in the Psalms, I'd like you to do a little exercise.

Extra Steps:

Select a group of ten psalms at random (e.g., 21–30 or 111–120) and skim through them, looking for verses that talk about God rescuing the psalmist or other people. These could be pleas for rescuing, or remembering times that God rescued someone, or affirmations about God being a rescuer. Find as many of these verses as you can. Then select one that's especially meaningful to you and spend a few minutes reflecting on how God has rescued you over the years.

> (Note: This is a good exercise to do with a group. Simply assign a different set of psalms to each person or pair of people. Afterwards, have each person share the verse they chose to focus on with the entire group.)

I hope that exercise helped you recall some situations where God has come to your rescue. Keep those in mind as we explore this theme. To help us understand more fully what it means that God is our Rescuer, let's look at Psalm 91. This Psalm of Trust focuses on the many ways that God rescues us. So, take a few moments and read through it, paying special attention to the different ways that God's rescuing is described. And, once again, I'll wait here for you.

* * *

This psalm's recounting of the extent and variety of God's rescuing is impressive, isn't it? Although the word "rescue" occurs only in verse 14, you probably noticed several related terms, such as "save" (v. 3), "protect" (v. 14), and "deliver" (v. 15). Those words imply an active intervention on God's part. In numerous ways the psalmist sees God stepping in to rescue his people, such as delivering them from "the fowler's snare" or "the deadly pestilence" (v. 3). Like when I came to Bella's rescue when she was being attacked, God comes to our rescue when we're under attack or in danger.

Even when we're not under attack or in immediate danger, however, God is still our Rescuer, but in a more preventive or protective way. We see this, for instance, in verse 2 with the images of "refuge" and "fortress." These two images represent places of safety and protection, and they're widely used in the book of Psalms, with God being referred to as a "refuge" some forty-three times and a "fortress" sixteen times. (The image of God as a "Rock" has a similar meaning and occurs some twenty-one times in the Psalms, often in combination with "refuge" or "fortress.")

In addition to those places of safety, Psalm 91 also compares God's protection to that of a mother bird keeping her chicks safe from danger by covering them with her wings (v. 4). God's protection even involves his angels, who are commanded to "guard you in all your ways" (v. 11). When we're abiding with God, we can know we're always safe and protected.

The images of "shield and rampart" in verse 3 are other ways of describing God's rescuing us by protecting us. These are military terms, and they're forms of protection against enemies. The use of "shield" is especially common throughout the Psalms. For example, in Psalm 3 David calls out to the Lord about the overwhelming number of his enemies, but he also realizes that God is "a shield around me," thus protecting him from those many enemies. Psalm 33:20 reflects both the active and passive aspects of God's rescuing: "We wait in hope for the Lord; he is our help and our shield." God is the One who will intervene when we need the help, but God also forms a protective shield around us at other times.

The author of Psalm 91 is confident that God will rescue his people from all sorts of dangers, including the traps and arrows of an enemy, diseases, battles, and wild animals. Furthermore, God will come to our rescue whether the danger occurs in the daytime or the middle of the night or any other time. There'll never be a time when God isn't watching over us and protecting us—and intervening when troubles and dangers do arise.

Occasionally, people have misinterpreted this psalm as saying that God's people won't experience bad things in life. They point to verses 9–10, which declare that, if we're dwelling with the Lord, "no harm will overtake you, no disaster will come near your tent." This would seem to imply that if we're in a proper relationship with God, we won't have troubles or problems in life. But that isn't what the psalm is promising. Notice verse 15. God says, "I will be with him in trouble." In other words, we should *expect* to be in trouble from time to time. Sometimes we may be caught in a fowler's snare. And life will have its terrors, and arrows, and pestilences. But in the midst of all life's troubles, God promises he'll always be with us. *That's* what the psalm promises. God will be with us, and God will rescue us. Of course, our rescue may not occur in this life, as Jesus' death on the cross reminds us. Or the stoning of Stephen (Acts 7). Or the sufferings and deaths of so many of God's people down through the centuries. But God does promise to be with us, to deliver us, to rescue us.

Knowing this ought to free us from the fears those troubles bring. For many people today, fear is a constant companion. That's understandable, since we live in a dangerous and violent world. Our world—and often our own personal experience—is marked by wars, terrorism, natural disasters, disease, prejudice, bullying, road rage, domestic violence, and much more. And God's people are victims of such things as often as other people. But Psalm 91 tells us we don't need to live in fear, because God is our Rescuer. We can trust that God will be with us in whatever troubles we experience. God will never stop watching over us, and nothing will ever separate us from him.

God doesn't just rescue us from the many troubles and problems we encounter in life. God also rescues us from our greatest problem: our own sinfulness. This is the central theme in seven psalms: 6, 32, 38, 51, 102, 130, and 143. Since at least the seventh century, the church has often called these the *Penitential Psalms*. Praying these psalms helps us recognize our sinfulness and creates in us a deep sorrow for our sin, but they also turn our hearts toward the only One who can forgive and cleanse us from our sin.

Of these seven Penitential Psalms, Psalm 51 is probably the best-known. This psalm's superscription says it was written after the prophet Nathan had confronted David about his affair with Bathsheba (2 Sam. 12). Although it would clearly fit such a context, the body of the psalm doesn't identify any particular sin, adultery or otherwise. Because of that, this psalm is widely used by individuals or groups for confessing any or all sin.

Although I often pray Psalm 51, the Penitential Psalm I turn to the most is Psalm 130. This is one of the Psalms of Ascent, which means God's people likely prayed it as they traveled to Jerusalem for the sacred festivals (see chapter 2). As the people walked towards the Holy City, they would've reflected on their own lack of holiness and how they needed God to rescue them from their sin. Take a moment and prayerfully read this brief psalm.

* * *

Like Psalm 51, Psalm 130 doesn't identify any particular sin that's troubling the psalmist. Instead, he's simply in "the depths" of spiritual and emotional despair (v. 1) and recognizes that his sin—whatever it might be—has put him in need of God's mercy and forgiveness. So he cries out to God. And then he waits. He waits perhaps for a word or a sense from God that he's been forgiven and can get back to worshiping and serving God.

The psalmist comes before God and makes his plea for mercy, because he knows that God is a loving God. Even when God's people are unfaithful, God remains faithful to the covenant he's made with them. The fact that they continue to exist and go about their lives is proof that God forgives them. Thus, the psalmist can dare to cry out for his own forgiveness from God.

I'm especially fascinated by two features in this short Lament. The first is the way the psalmist moves from the sorrow for his own sin into a plea for all of Israel to follow his example and lament over their sinfulness as well. He understands that we're all sinners—each and every one of us—and we all need to be rescued from our sin. At any given moment we may not feel like we're in "the depths" of sin, but we always stand in need of God's mercy and forgiveness. So there's something very right about acknowledging our sin together. We're a community of sinners, and together we can cry out to God. I appreciate the psalmist's reminder about this communal dimension in confessing our sin.

The other fascinating feature is the psalmist's understanding of redemption in verses 7–8. The Psalms frequently portray God as Israel's Redeemer. The title "Redeemer" is only used twice (in Psalms 19:14 and 78:35), but numerous other psalms describe God as redeeming his people by rescuing them from enemies and other forms of danger (see, e.g., Psalms 49:15, 77:15, 103:4, and 111:9). In Psalm 130, the "enemy" is sin, and redemption is God's way of rescuing his people from their sin.

In Old Testament times redemption always meant more than merely saving someone from a dangerous situation. While redemption certainly involved some form of deliverance, it also always included the payment of a price. So, for instance, first-born sons were redeemed by the parents paying five shekels to the priest (Num. 18:14–16), and property that had been sold could be redeemed, or bought back, by a kinsman-redeemer (Lev. 25:23–34). Thus, when God rescues people by redeeming them, it implies that God is paying a price of some kind in order to get them back.

We need to keep this in mind when we read verse 8 in Psalm 130. The psalmist has added an extra pronoun to emphasize that God personally is the One who will pay the price for this redemption: "He *himself* will redeem Israel from all their sins." For Israel to be rescued from their sin, a price needed to be paid. But, thanks be to God, God himself was willing to pay it. That's the message the psalmist wants his fellow Israelites to understand and respond to: God loves them so much that he's willing to do whatever is necessary to rescue them from all their sin.

For the psalmist, God's redemption of Israel was a joyful word of promise and hope. But, for those of us who are Christians, we look back to the sacrifice of Jesus as the fulfillment of that promise. In the person of Jesus Christ, God himself entered the world on the greatest rescue mission of all. God came to redeem not just Israel, but all of humanity, from their sin. And the price to obtain this redemption was Jesus' death on the cross. At Calvary, the Son of God—God himself in human flesh—died as humanity's redemption price. God paid the price himself to rescue us from our sin and bring us back to himself. Perhaps the Apostle Paul had Psalm 130 in mind when he wrote, "For he has rescued us from the dominion of darkness and brought us into the kingdom of the Son he loves, in whom we have redemption, the forgiveness of sins" (Col. 1:13–14). Jesus is God's ultimate rescue act, and the Psalms prepare us for that with their emphasis on God as our Rescuer.

Extra Steps:

The first question in the Heidelberg Catechism asks, "What is your only comfort, in life and in death?" As the answer, it declares, "That I belong—body and soul, in life and in death—not to myself but to my faithful Savior, Jesus Christ, who at the cost of his own blood has fully paid for all my sins. . . . Therefore, by his Holy Spirit, he also assures me of eternal life, and makes me wholeheartedly willing and ready from now on to live for him."

Reflect on what it means to you personally that Jesus has paid the redemption price to rescue you from your sin. Can you confess these words of the Catechism as your own? If you can't, why not ask God to give you this assurance that you belong to him because of what Jesus has done for you?

What does it mean for you to live wholeheartedly for Jesus, your Rescuer?

In our examination of Psalms 91 and 130 we've only sampled a few of the ways that God rescues his people. Consider those two psalms to be like the special dog treats I sometimes give to Emma and Bella. *Yummmm!* However, even in this brief treatment, we've seen that, as our Rescuer, God delivers us from life's troubles, surrounds us and protects us like a refuge or a shield, and forgives and redeems us from our sin. As you continue to explore the book of Psalms on your own, your eyes will be opened to more and more ways that God relates to you as your Rescuer.

What kind of response should this call forth from us? How ought we to respond to God as our Rescuer? Earlier in this chapter, I said that God as our Creator calls for wholehearted worship and God as our Leader calls for faithful obedience. I would suggest that God as our Rescuer calls for *grateful love.*

If we have any lingering doubts about God's love for us when we think of God as our Creator and our Leader, surely those have been erased by God's actions as our Rescuer. In countless ways, the Psalms affirm God's unfailing love for us. With such love surrounding us, how can we not respond with our own love, however feeble it might be? We've done nothing to earn that divine love; it's simply God's gift to us—a gift we receive with joy and gratitude. But that's all our Rescuer asks from us: that we give him our heart in grateful love. What a joyful privilege!

This chapter, this panoramic overview of the Psalms, began by stating that the purpose of God's Prayer Book is "to draw us into a deeper and more vibrant relationship with God." Understanding that God is our Creator is where it all begins, because then we know that God created us for himself and we belong to him. But the Psalms also show us that God is our Leader, who wants to have an ongoing relationship with us and who therefore calls us to follow him and obey his ways as he leads us along our life's journey.

Faithful obedience and wholehearted worship arise naturally from those two ways that God relates to us. But when we experience God as our Rescuer—and experience it over and over and over—that's when grateful love grows in our heart. In all of these ways, then, we enter into a closer and more intimate walk with God. Our life becomes a holy walk with the God who is our Creator, our Leader, and our Rescuer. Let it be so, Lord, let it be so.

Extra Steps:

Reflect on each of God's three ways of relating to us, as we've discussed in this panoramic overview of the Psalms. What does it mean to you that God is your Creator? Your Leader? Your Rescuer?

Then consider your response to God:

- *Are you worshiping God wholeheartedly? How might you deepen your worship of God?*
- *Are you faithfully obeying God? Where in your life might you be resisting God's authority and leadership?*
- *Are you walking in grateful love for all that God has done for you? What can you give thanks to God for right now?*

Next Steps

*"Praise the L*ORD*.*
Praise God in his sanctuary;
praise him in his mighty heavens.
Praise him for his acts of power;
praise him for his surpassing greatness.
Praise him with the sounding of the trumpet;
praise him with the harp and lyre,
praise him with timbrel and dancing,
praise him with the strings and pipe,
praise him with the clash of cymbals,
praise him with resounding cymbals.
*Let everything that has breath praise the L*ORD*.*
*Praise the L*ORD*."*

—PSALM 150

COULD THERE BE A more appropriate psalm to use for this concluding section? Psalm 150 serves as a doxology for the book of Psalms, and it reminds us that our ultimate reason for praying the Psalms is so that we might praise and honor God with our entire being for ever and ever. So I want these words that close the book of Psalms to echo in your mind as you contemplate your next steps with the Psalms.

My hope is that you've been drawn to the Psalms in new ways as you've worked your way through this book. I also hope that you've been encouraged to pray the Psalms on your own, perhaps incorporating either or both of the supporting spiritual practices I've described: prayer-walking and heart-learning. I believe those two practices will significantly enhance your experience in learning and praying the Psalms.

However, like any new endeavor, learning and praying the Psalms will require some work and effort on your part. Thomas Merton reminds us of this in his book, *Praying the Psalms,* when he says "we need zeal and strength and perseverance" if we're going to lay hands on the blessings that are in the Psalms. Then Merton offers this encouragement:

> In the last analysis, it is not so much what we get out of the Psalms that rewards us, as what we put into them. If we really make them our prayer, really prefer them to other methods and expedients, in order to let God pray in us in His own words, and if we sincerely desire above all to offer Him this particularly pure homage of our Christian faith, then indeed we will enter into the meaning of the Psalms, and they will become our favorite vocal prayers.[1]

If you've decided to take on this challenge of learning and praying the Psalms, where should you begin? What next steps might you take? Here are some suggestions.

First, recognize that God himself has placed in your heart and mind this desire to pray the Psalms. So begin by thanking God for that desire and asking God to guide you as you cultivate this spiritual practice. Prayer is always a response to God, and as you begin your work with the Psalms, you will simply be praying back to God words that God's already spoken to you. Embrace this truth, and tell God that you're looking forward to getting to know him better as his words become written in your mind and heart.

Second, as you've read this book, has there been a psalm that spoke to you in a special way? Did you have a *Wow!* moment or an *Aha!* experience as you read and reflected on one of the psalms? If you did, then that's the psalm you should start with. Otherwise, choose one that's already a favorite of yours, or consider beginning with Psalm 1, 8, 19, 95, 100, or 121 (these psalms are fairly short but also have themes that fit well with the spiritual practices of prayer-walking and heart-learning). Follow the steps described in chapter 3 for heart-learning a psalm. Make up your flashcards, and begin memorizing and heart-learning the psalm you've chosen. God has already

---

1. Merton, *Praying the Psalms,* 44–45.

spoken to you in the words of that particular psalm, and now you're ready to begin praying those words back to God.

Third, be patient with yourself as you get started. If you haven't done this kind of memorizing recently (or ever), it may take a while to get the hang of it. But you *can* do it! And when you do get one psalm memorized, use it as a *daily* prayer, so that you'll begin heart-learning it as well.

Fourth, when you sense the Spirit nudging you to start learning a second psalm, add that to your collection as well. Then pray *both* of those psalms each day. Keep on learning new psalms as you're able and as the Spirit inspires you. On average, I've memorized a new psalm about every four to six weeks. However, I've never set a goal to reach a certain number. I just take on a new psalm when one speaks to me in a special way or when I find myself praying my current psalms too routinely. Learning a new psalm often refreshes my interest in the ones I've learned previously.

As you consider your next steps, let me share one last dog-walking story with you.

As Emma and I walked through the nature preserve near our home, I led us away from our usual routes and discovered a trail we had never taken before, one that appeared to lead up the side of the bluff. For some time, I'd wanted to find a trail that led all the way up to Five Mile Prairie, the neighborhood that lies at the top of the bluff. So, excitement gripped me as I thought, "Perhaps this is it!"

As we walked along, however, the trail became steeper and steeper. Soon Emma and I were scrambling up over rocks, with me grabbing onto branches to help with my balance. After a while, I realized I would never be able to go back down this same trail. So we kept pressing onward and upward. Eventually, we clambered over the top edge of the bluff and into the backyard of one of the beautiful homes that overlook the nature preserve a couple hundred feet below. We'd found our way to the top!

Of course, now we had to find our way back home—and the way we'd come was not an option.

Have you ever felt lost even though you knew exactly where you were? That's how I was feeling. I knew right where my home was—it was down there at the bottom of the bluff. I just didn't know how to get *down there*. So Emma and I headed off, walking along the edge of the bluff, as I looked for another route down. After another fifteen or twenty minutes of walking, I found a trail that headed down the hillside—one we could actually negotiate. So down we went, following the switchbacks as we descended lower and lower. Finally, Emma and I arrived back home again—after a much longer walk than we had planned.

I like that story, because it reminds me that we don't always know where our journeys are going to take us. We set off in some direction, thinking we know where we're going. But then the path takes us someplace very different and unexpected—yet a place filled with new adventures and fun experiences.

If you're hesitating about embarking on your own journey with the Psalms, I hope you'll allow that story to embolden you to take the first steps. Your journey may resemble my journey in some ways, but it will also become your own unique journey in many other ways. God will lead you along different trails on your holy walks. Yet wherever God takes you in your journey with the Psalms, you can be confident you will draw closer to God's heart.

But, of course, that won't happen unless you take those first steps along the trail.

My journey began with a single psalm, Psalm 145. At the time I didn't even recognize it as the beginning of a trail or a journey, much less have any idea where it would lead me. I just thought I was preparing my next sermon. But now, several years and many steps later, I'm still following that trail. I'm still on this journey, which continues to bring new adventures with the Psalms, fresh insights into life, and a deeper walk with my Lord. After all this time, I'm still not an expert on the Psalms—but I'm learning. When it comes to holy walks, perhaps I am—and always will be—simply a "journeyman" (pun fully intended). But, thanks be to God, what a great journey it's been.

I hope you'll join me on it.

Well, Emma's asking to go out for another walk. But before we go, please allow me to offer a prayer for all of us as we engage in our holy walks with the Psalms:

> *Gracious God, you created us to be your people and we belong to you. You lead us in your ways, fulfilling the purposes of your heart in us and through us. And you rescue us again and again, as we stray from your ways and as our enemies—human or otherwise—rise up against us. Thank you for calling us on this incredible journey with you, and I ask that you would help us always to make that journey in company with you. Guide our thoughts, words, and actions so that our lives can truly be holy walks. Thank you also for the gift of the Psalms. May these words, inspired by your Holy Spirit, fill our*

hearts and minds, shaping our prayers and shaping our very selves. Now, Loving Lord, I thank you, in particular, for the person reading these words. I ask you to bless them with your grace and peace, fill their heart with love for you, and enable them to always walk closely with you. May you receive all the praise, honor, and glory! Amen.

Extra Steps:

Reflect back on why you decided to read this book. What did you expect to get out of it? How were those expectations met (or not met)?

What surprises did you encounter as you learned about the Psalms and holy walks?

What was one important thing you learned about the Psalms? About prayer? About holy walks?

What next step is God asking you to take at this point in your walk with him?

Appendix

The Psalms I'm Heart-Learning . . .

I KNOW WHEN I'VE memorized a psalm: I can recite it easily and flawlessly without looking at my flashcards. But when have I *heart-learned* a psalm? That's much harder to answer, and perhaps that's a task that one never fully accomplishes. Heart-learning means the psalm is written on my heart, not just in the memory banks of my brain. As I continue to pray these psalms—long after I've memorized them—the Spirit etches the words deeper and deeper into my heart. And thus, in that way, I believe God continues to work in the innermost parts of my soul.

I'm providing this list as a work-in-progress to help you know about my journey. Your psalms and your journey will be different, of course, but my hope is that this might encourage you on your own holy walks. Start with one psalm and see where it takes you. Here's a look at where God has taken me. Thus far.

Psalm 1—I memorized this for a sermon I gave for a Youth Sunday worship service. During the previous several months, the students had been learning about the psalm's theme of being like a tree firmly planted by streams of water. I often use this psalm at the beginning of my walks.

Psalm 3—A good psalm for those times when life feels a bit overwhelming.

Psalm 5—A "morning psalm," I chose to memorize this one because so many of my prayer-walks are in the early-morning hours.

Psalm 8—In January 2012, the Rev. Dr. Trygve Johnson brought this psalm alive for me in a special way when he preached on it as part of a series on the Psalms during a worship service at Hope College. This was the third psalm I memorized, and I was beginning to sense a special place developing in my heart for the Psalms.

APPENDIX: THE PSALMS I'M HEART-LEARNING . . .

Psalm 13—The Rev. Frank Thomas introduced this psalm to me in his sermon at the Calvin College *Symposium on Worship* in January 2012. I was fascinated by his insights into the abrupt shift from the complaints of verses 1–4 to the praises in verses 5–6 (see chapter 7). This was the first time I truly began to understand the purpose for the Psalms of Lament.

Psalm 15—I'm intrigued by the simple format of this psalm and what we learn about what matters to God.

Psalm 16—A wonderful psalm about expressing gratitude for one's life. I memorized this one because I felt I needed to learn to be more grateful (see chapter 6).

Psalm 19—An old favorite of mine, I especially appreciate the psalmist's obvious delight in God's Word.

Psalm 23—I memorized this much-beloved psalm while I was ministering to an elderly woman who was in hospice care. I prayed this psalm with her at the end of most of my visits with her, and we also used it in her funeral service (see chapter 3).

Psalm 25—I memorized this in the *New Living Translation*. The psalm has two very distinct (and different) parts. I'm still trying to figure out how they're connected.

Psalm 27—I was drawn to the psalmist's courage in facing life's fearful situations. Waiting for the Lord (final verse) is extremely hard for me to do, but something we all need to do.

Psalm 30—This Psalm of Thanksgiving helps me reflect on the many ways God has blessed me and answered my prayers over the years.

Psalm 32—This psalm is a prayer of confession for sin, but it also reminds me of the foolishness of trying to hide my sin from God. Better to just confess it and accept God's forgiveness.

Psalm 33—This Praise Psalm presents numerous reasons for praising our great God.

Psalm 34—A Wisdom Psalm that contrasts the righteous with those who do evil, it shows how the Lord is close to those who look to him and seek to follow his ways.

Psalm 40—The psalmist opens with, "I waited patiently for the Lord." Waiting patiently for anything, even the Lord, has never been easy for me. That was a sufficient reason to learn this psalm.

Psalm 46—I use this psalm frequently when I make pastoral visits.

Psalm 47—I decided to memorize this psalm when Pastor Jud Marvel, the lead pastor at one of the churches I served, announced he was going to preach on it as part of an Ascension Day worship service.

Psalm 51—Similar to Psalm 47, I chose to memorize this next psalm when Pastor Jud told me he was going to spend three weeks preaching on it. It just seemed like a good thing to do. This psalm is a good reminder for me that I can't hide my sin from God—but also that God is a very merciful and forgiving God.

Psalm 63—Another psalm I often use on pastoral calls, especially in the case of serious illness (v. 9: "those who want to kill me") where I remind people that one day God will destroy everything that harms us, including disease.

Psalm 65—Although this isn't a Creation Psalm, it's certainly an Environmental Psalm. Think of it as an Eco-Psalm. The emphasis on God's care for the world he created is a major reason I decided to learn this psalm.

Psalm 67—I was attracted to this psalm by its similarity to a benediction I frequently offer at the end of worship services (Num. 6:24–26).

Psalm 71—This psalm was part of a study guide I was using with my small group. The topic: "Growing Older and Wiser." Read the psalm and you'll see how well it fits.

Psalm 73—I admire the psalmist's honesty in recounting his struggles with doubt. Over the years I've wrestled with many of those same thoughts, and I greatly appreciate his personal testimony of faith in the midst of doubts.

Psalm 84—A long-time favorite of mine, this was probably the fifth or sixth psalm I memorized. I had preached on it in the past and often used it in pastoral care situations, so it seemed natural to go ahead and begin heart-learning it.

APPENDIX: THE PSALMS I'M HEART-LEARNING . . .

Psalm 86—I discovered this psalm while I was reading around in the book of Psalms. I'm not sure why I never really noticed it before, but this time I was impressed with this humble psalm and knew I wanted to make it one of my prayers.

Psalm 88—Perhaps the darkest of all the psalms, I memorized this for a Darkest Night service at our church. I expected it to be rather depressing, but instead found it surprisingly encouraging. Brueggemann calls this psalm "a model for unanswered prayer."[1]

Psalm 90—I preached on this psalm years ago and especially appreciate the prayer, "Teach us to number our days, that we may gain a heart of wisdom" (v. 12).

Psalm 91—We live in a time when so many people seem to be afraid of so many things. This psalm reminds me of where my true security lies (see chapter 9).

Psalm 92—I was drawn to this psalm by one verse in particular. I'll leave it to you to figure out which verse that was, but I'll give you a clue: we're all getting older.

Psalm 95—We once discussed this psalm during a church staff meeting, where I learned that it's a daily prayer for Benedictine monks. The abrupt shift near the end of verse 7 underscores the need for both worship and obedience.

Psalm 98—A beautiful Psalm of Praise, I especially like it in the *English Standard Version*.

Psalm 100—A wonderful psalm to use as a Call To Worship, I memorized this on one occasion for just that reason.

Psalm 103—I served in two churches where this psalm was used regularly as part of a thanksgiving prayer in their Communion liturgy.

Psalm 104—This psalm was assigned as pre-reading for a workshop I attended that was led by Old Testament scholar Walter Brueggemann. I found the psalm to be so fascinating that I started memorizing it prior to the workshop. Unfortunately, I didn't have enough time to complete it before the workshop, but I did finish it shortly afterwards.

1. Brueggemann, *No Secrets*, 113.

APPENDIX: THE PSALMS I'M HEART-LEARNING . . .

Psalm 105—In the past I probably would have skimmed through or skipped this Sacred Story Psalm, but I'm coming to appreciate it so much as a synopsis of God's work in creating a people for himself—a people that I am privileged to be part of.

Psalm 119—People sometimes ask if I've memorized this psalm, the longest one in the Bible. Well, I'm working on it! I'm approaching it as though each of the twenty-two stanzas were a separate psalm, and then learning it stanza by stanza.

Psalm 121- A Psalm of Ascent, this is one of my favorite "walking" psalms. This is also one that I use frequently in pastoral care situations.

Psalm 126—Another Psalm of Ascent, I always feel a bit more joyful after praying this one.

Psalm 130—A wonderful psalm about God's mercy and forgiveness.

Psalm 131—I was drawn to this very short psalm when I heard it read during a morning prayer service. I especially appreciate its image of a quiet heart waiting in hope for God. Incidentally, this is the only psalm I've memorized using *The Message*. I usually find *The Message* to be too colloquial for memorizing, although it's often helpful in understanding particular psalms.

Psalm 134—I memorized this short psalm when I happened across an online video about memorizing Scripture by Dr. Tim Brown (see chapter 3).

Psalm 138—This psalm was used in a Psalmic Worship Service that I attended at Whitworth University, and I was moved by the psalmist's expression of praise for God.

Psalm 139—A favorite psalm for many of us, although verses 19–22 are rarely cited.

Psalm 143—Verse 8 had been a regular prayer of mine for a long time. I eventually got around to memorizing the entire psalm.

Psalm 145—This was the first psalm I memorized (see chapter 1). I didn't realize it at the time, but this is the one that got me started on my journey into praying the Psalms.

APPENDIX: THE PSALMS I'M HEART-LEARNING . . .

Psalm 148—One of the "Hallelujah Psalms," I like the way the psalmist invites all of creation—including the animals and plants, and even the weather—to join in praising our Creator.

Psalm 150—This psalm serves as a doxology for the entire book of Psalms, and it just seemed appropriate for me to add it to my list. I often pray this psalm at the end of my walks.

Bibliography

Listed below are works cited in this book, as well as additional books and references which have shaped my thinking about the Psalms, prayer, and spiritual practices. I am indebted to each of these authors.

Anderson, A. A. *Psalms, Vols. 1 and 2 (New Century Bible series)*. Somerset, England: Oliphants, 1972.
Anderson, Bernhard W. *Out of the Depths: The Psalms Speak for Us Today, 3rd ed.* Louisville, KY: Westminster John Knox, 2000.
Anderson, Keith R. *A Spirituality of Listening: Living What We Hear*. Downers Grove, IL: InterVarsity, 2016.
Baab, Lynne M. *Joy Together: Spiritual Practices for Your Congregation*. Downers Grove, IL: InterVarsity, 2012.
———. *The Power of Listening: Building Skills for Mission and Ministry*. Lanham, MD: Rowman & Littlefield, 2014.
———. *A Renewed Spirituality: Finding Fresh Paths at Midlife*. Downers Grove, IL: InterVarsity, 2002.
Billings, J. Todd. *Rejoicing in Lament: Wrestling with Incurable Cancer and Life in Christ*. Grand Rapids, MI: Brazos, 2015.
Bonhoeffer, Dietrich. *Psalms: The Prayer Book of the Bible*. Minneapolis: Augsburg Fortress, 1970.
Brueggemann, Walter. *From Whom No Secrets Are Hid: Introducing the Psalms*. Louisville, KY: Westminster John Knox, 2014.
———. *The Message of the Psalms: A Theological Commentary*. Minneapolis: Augsburg Fortress, 1984.
———. *Praying the Psalms: Engaging Scripture and the Life of the Spirit, 2nd ed.* Eugene, OR: Wipf and Stock, 2007.
———. *The Psalms and the Life of Faith*, edited by Patrick D. Miller. Minneapolis: Fortress, 1995.
Brueggemann, Walter, and William H. Bellinger, Jr. *Psalms (New Cambridge Bible Commentary)*. New York: Cambridge University Press, 2014.
Buechner, Frederick. *Telling the Truth: The Gospel as Tragedy, Comedy, and Fairy Tale*. New York: HarperCollins, 1977.

BIBLIOGRAPHY

Bullock, C. Hassell. *Encountering the Book of Psalms: A Literary and Theological Introduction.* Grand Rapids, MI: Baker Academic, 2001.

Card, Michael. *A Sacred Sorrow: Reaching Out to God in the Lost Language of Lament.* Colorado Springs, CO: NavPress, 2005.

Davis, Ken. *Lighten Up!* Grand Rapids, MI: Zondervan, 2000.

Eldredge, John. *Walking with God.* Nashville, TN: Thomas Nelson, 2008.

Foster, Richard J. *Sanctuary of the Soul: Journey into Meditative Prayer.* Downers Grove, IL: InterVarsity, 2011.

Griggs, Donald L. *Discovering the Psalms: Passion, Promise & Praise – Leader's Guide.* Pittsburgh, PA: The Kerygma Program, 1993.

———. *Discovering the Psalms: Passion, Promise & Praise – Resource Book.* Pittsburgh, PA: The Kerygma Program, 1993.

———. *Preaching and Teaching the Psalms.* Nashville, TN: Abingdon, 1984.

Hallesby, O. *Prayer.* Minneapolis: Augsburg, 1931.

Hansen, David. *Long Wandering Prayer: An Invitation To Walk with God.* Downers Grove, IL: InterVarsity, 2001.

Harrison, R.K. *Introduction to the Old Testament.* Grand Rapids, MI: Eerdmans, 1969.

Hunter, Alistair G. *An Introduction to the Psalms.* London: T & T Clark, 2007.

Hybels, Bill. *Too Busy Not To Pray.* Downers Grove, IL: InterVarsity, 1988.

Jacoby, Matthew. *Deeper Places: Experiencing God in the Psalms.* Grand Rapids, MI: Baker, 2013.

Keller, Timothy. *Prayer: Experiencing Awe and Intimacy with God.* New York: Penguin Random House, 2014.

Lamott, Anne. *Help, Thanks, Wow: The Three Essential Prayers.* New York: Riverhead, 2012.

Lewis, C. S. *A Grief Observed.* New York: Bantam, 1961.

———. *Reflections on the Psalms.* New York: Houghton Mifflin Harcourt, 1958.

Longman III, Tremper. *How To Read the Psalms.* Downers Grove, IL: InterVarsity, 1988.

———. *Psalms (Tyndale Old Testament Commentary).* Downers Grove, IL: InterVarsity, 2014.

Lucas, Ernest C. *Exploring the Old Testament, Vol. 3: A Guide to the Psalms and Wisdom Literature.* Downers Grove, IL: InterVarsity, 2003.

Mays, James L. *Psalms (Interpretation).* Louisville, KY: Westminster John Knox, 1994.

Merton, Thomas. *Praying the Psalms.* Collegeville, MN: The Liturgical Press, 1956.

Miller, Calvin. *The Path of Celtic Prayer: An Ancient Way to Everyday Joy.* Downers Grove, IL: InterVarsity, 2007.

Okholm, Dennis. *Monk Habits for Everyday People: Benedictine Spirituality for Protestants.* Grand Rapids, MI: Brazos, 2007.

Ortberg, John. *God Is Closer Than You Think.* Grand Rapids, MI: Zondervan, 2005.

———. *The Life You've Always Wanted.* Grand Rapids, MI: Zondervan, 2002.

Patterson, Ben. *God's Prayer Book: The Power and Pleasure of Praying the Psalms.* Carol Stream, IL: Tyndale House.

Pemberton, Glenn. *After Lament: Psalms for Learning To Trust Again.* Abilene, TX: Abilene Christian University Press, 2014.

———. *Hurting with God: Learning To Lament with the Psalms.* Abilene, TX: Abilene Christian University Press, 2012.

Peterson, Eugene H. *Answering God: The Psalms As Tools for Prayer.* New York: HarperCollins, 1989.

———. *Eat This Book: A Conversation in the Art of Spiritual Reading.* Grand Rapids, MI: Eerdmans, 2006.

———. *Leap Over a Wall: Earthy Spirituality for Everyday Christians.* New York: HarperCollins, 1997.

———. *A Long Obedience in the Same Direction: Discipleship in an Instant Society,* 2nd ed. Downers Grove, IL: InterVarsity, 2000.

Rinker, Rosalind. *Prayer: Conversing with God.* Grand Rapids, MI: Zondervan, 1959.

Sire, James W. *Learning To Pray Through the Psalms.* Downers Grove, IL: InterVarsity, 2005.

Towns, Elmer. *Praying the Psalms: To Touch God and Be Touched by Him.* Shippensburg, PA: Destiny Image, 2004.

Wenham, Gordon. *Psalms as Torah: Reading Biblical Song Ethically.* Grand Rapids, MI: Baker Academic, 2012.

———. *The Psalter Reclaimed: Praying and Praising with the Psalms.* Wheaton, IL: Crossway, 2013.

Willard, Dallas. *Hearing God: Developing a Conversational Relationship with God.* Downers Grove, IL: InterVarsity, 2012.

Witvliet, John D. *The Biblical Psalms in Christian Worship: A Brief Introduction and Guide to Resources.* Grand Rapids, MI: Eerdmans, 2007.

Wright, N. T. *The Case for the Psalms: Why They Are Essential.* New York: HarperCollins, 2013.

Yancey, Philip. *The Bible Jesus Read: Why the Old Testament Matters.* Grand Rapids, MI: Zondervan, 1999.

———. *Prayer: Does It Make a Difference?* Grand Rapids, MI: Zondervan, 2006.

www.ingramcontent.com/pod-product-compliance
Lightning Source LLC
Chambersburg PA
CBHW071232170426
43191CB00032B/1354